# EARLY ENGLISH PARLIAMENTS

High Courts, Royal Councils, or Representative Assemblies?

PROBLEMS IN EUROPEAN CIVILIZATION

# EARLY ENGLISH PARLIAMENTS

## High Courts, Royal Councils, or Representative Assemblies?

EDITED WITH AN INTRODUCTION BY

*Gerald P. Bodet*

LOUISIANA STATE UNIVERSITY
IN NEW ORLEANS

D. C. HEATH AND COMPANY
Lexington, Massachusetts  Toronto  London

Library of Congress Catalog Card Number 67–29336

Copyright © 1968 by D. C. Heath and Company

# Table of Contents

# Introduction

URING THE REIGN OF HENRY III the word "parliament" was used interchangeably with "great council" and "colloquy" to indicate a large gathering of crown and magnates for the discussion of important business. Gradually it crowded out other terms and took on a special significance, describing, as Sir Maurice Powicke has observed, "the king in council in a gathering of wider scope." Then at the end of Henry's reign, in the midst of war and revolution, representatives of the less politically powerful social groups, the knights and townsmen, were summoned to a parliament. For the next half century these groups attended sporadically, sometimes answering royal requests for taxes, and other times petitioning the king for special favors. Meanwhile crown and magnates remained at the center of parliamentary activities. Another era of baronial-led revolution commenced in 1311, and at its close the direct professional influence of the crown officials in parliamentary affairs had diminished. After 1327 the representative elements were never absent from parliament; by 1340 they were physically separated from the magnates and their petitions were becoming more and more identified with legislation. Parliament as an institution had emerged.

The events just described seem clear enough; in modern times they have received closer attention than any other events in English history. Yet a constitutional historian, Colin Rhys Lovell, wrote in 1962 "that probably no other aspect of the modern English constitution is lost in quite the same obscurity." T. F. T. Pluck-nett expressed the same sentiment in 1940, when he declared that "no English institution has been studied with such ardor, and with so little definite result, as parliament." These comments, coming over a half century after Stubbs and Maitland wrote, and following upon decades of extensive research by twentieth century scholars, underline the complex nature of the search for parliamentary origins.

A work such as this, containing only a few selected articles from the burgeoning bibliography of parliamentary history, can approach only some aspects of the subject. Accordingly, the period covered has been limited to the reigns of Henry III and Edward I, and the emphasis placed upon parliamentary business and parliamentary representation. The selections have been organized in three parts, treating (I) the business of parliaments, (II) the summoning of representatives, and (III) the influence of contemporary European practices upon England.

Part I is concerned with the question, were early parliaments assemblies convened for purposes of high politics, or were they occasions during which judicial and administrative business was conducted? In attempting to answer this question, historians have been confronted with a problem of terminology: the word "parliament" was only one of several terms used by the thirteenth century man to describe assemblies very similar in function and composition. Today we can easily identify the sittings at Westminster as meetings of Her Majesty's Parliament, but the subjects of Henry III and Edward I saw the king at

Westminster, at Gloucester, at Lincoln, or at Northampton, holding "parliaments," "colloquies," and "great councils," during which he promulgated laws, levied taxes, dispensed justice, and held state trials. Attending these gatherings were barons and prelates, and from time to time, knights and burgesses, all variously summoned. "to treat," "to give counsel," "to ordain and do," "to have a conference," "to counsel and consent," and "to do what shall be ordained."

Which of these meetings were parliaments and which not? Which activities were typical of a parliamentary gathering and which groups of people must necessarily be present? And finally, was parliament at this stage a definite assembly, or was it merely an occasion during which diverse business was conducted? To William Stubbs and the school of nineteenth century Whig-national historians[1] who traced English parliamentary assemblies to an Anglo-Saxon urge for self-government, and saw that urge expressed by the barons in 1265, fulfilled by Edward I in 1295, and confirmed by the same king in 1297, thirteenth-century parliaments were not mere "occasions"; they were national assemblies, as central to the medieval constitution as the nineteenth-century parliament was central to the Victorian constitution. And the continuity of parliamentary growth since

[1] The Whig-national school of nineteenth-century historians, Henry Hallam, T. B. Macaulay, E. A. Freeman, and J. R. Green, considered parliament a pre-Norman institution and viewed the Conquest (and strong monarchy) as disruptive of parliamentary evolution. These premises had originally been the stock-in-trade of seventeenth-century parliamentary propagandists like Sir Edward Coke, who failed to understand the intimate connection between Norman feudalism, the king's council, and parliament. For a discussion of seventeenth-century attitudes toward parliamentary origins, see J. G. A. Pocock, *The Ancient Constitution and the Fundamental Law* (Cambridge, 1957), and Quentin Skinner, "History and Ideology in the English Revolution," *The Historical Journal*, VIII (1965), 151–179. "Whig history," in the general sense, means reading contemporary values into a past age; for a stinging critique of this method of studying the past, see H. Butterfield, *The Whig Interpretation of History* (London, 1931, Norton edition, New York, 1965).

the Middle Ages explained the comparative English political serenity at moments of European revolutionary chaos in 1830, 1848, and 1870.

In the three-volume *Constitutional History of England,* published in 1878 (selection number one), Stubbs distinguished parliaments from less important gatherings of crown and magnates by the presence of the three estates — clergy, barons, and commons — and by the evidence of activities typical of national assemblies: the levying of taxes, the promulgation of statutes, and the consideration of state matters. For Stubbs, the parliament of 1295 best fitted this description and was therefore a "Model Parliament," "serving as the pattern for all future assemblies of the nation." When Edward I tried to narrow the authority of parliament by levying taxes without its advice, the barons, Stubbs's "heroes of the thirteenth century," forced the king in 1297 to confirm the Charters and recognize parliament's tax-granting powers. From that moment, Stubbs wrote, "English liberty may be considered achieved."

Though some of this may be dismissed as blatant Anglo-Saxon nationalism, Stubbs's presentation was more balanced than his critics admit. Cautioning that "the parliamentary constitution was by no means the whole of the English system," he drew a picture as accurate as existing sources would allow of a vigorous monarchical establishment. While parliament was being created, the vitality of the royal government "remained unimpaired" and grew "side by side with the . . . power of parliament." The king's council continued to provide extraordinary judicial remedies for the subject, handling a multitude of petitions and judicial cases. Statute-making frequently involved "participation of the council as well as that of the assembled estates," and occasionally king and council made ordinances which were "received as of full and equal authority" with parliamentary legislation. In all this there can be seen a strong hint of that fusion of powers in the central administration which would be stressed by the followers of Maitland, but Stubbs's system as a whole focused upon parliament and left the role of the royal administration tantalizingly vague.

Recognizing the imbalance of Stubbs's emphasis, twentieth-century historians turned their attention to the royal administration. Studies of the king's council, the royal wardrobe, the courts, and other central offices revealed the complexity of Angevin government and indicated that parliament, far from dominating the medieval scene, was itself overshadowed by the administration. At the same time, the new research made it clear that medieval government could not be departmentalized into sharply defined agencies; council, courts, and parliament were part of an interlocking system with overlapping functions and personnel.

The degree to which parliament shared the personnel and functions of the royal council was first illustrated by Frederick William Maitland in his "Introduction" to the *Memoranda de Parliamento, 1305,* published by the Rolls Series in 1893. Though he maintained he was not "departing very far from the path marked out by books that are already classical," Maitland provided the initial evidence for a revision of Stubbs's system when he suggested that parliamentary business consisted largely in the handling of petitions. Others, including Stubbs, had noted the petitioning procedures of the 1305 parliament, but had considered them activities of the king's council, not parliament. Maitland (selection number two), called the king's council the "core and essence" of the 1305 parliament. The royal officials were the directing agents, and representatives stood unobtrusively in the background, petitioning the crown for justice and then retiring while king and council, still in a gathering called a parliament, discussed the great affairs of state. *Fleta,* the anonymous legal commentator of Edward I's reign, had put it rightly when he said, "the king has . . . his court in his council in his parliaments, when there are present prelates, earls, barons, magnates and other learned men. And there doubts are determined regarding judgments, new remedies are devised for wrongs newly brought to light, and . . . justice dispensed to everyone according to his deserts."

Although Maitland's "Introduction" excited little controversy at first, it pointed to the council as a whole new field of inquiry for the origins of parliament. Charles H. McIlwain argued (selection number three) that parliament was a court, engaged in the same judicial activities as the king's council, before it was a legislature. Historians who referred to parliament as a political assembly were introducing to the Middle Ages modern ideas about "separation of powers" and missing altogether the reality of the fusion of agencies and functions which characterized medieval government. They were also forgetting the importance of the fundamental law, a reservoir of ancient tradition which needed only to be reinterpreted to meet changing conditions. "Legislation" was in fact the declaration of fundamental law by the king's judges, not the enactment of new law by parliamentary representatives. On this last point, legal historians like T. F. T. Plucknett have criticized McIlwain, demonstrating that Edward I did enact fresh legislation to meet changed social and economic conditions. Although they agree that the king, and not parliament, framed these early statutes, critics insist that the fundamental law did not, and could not, "defeat" new legislation as "repugnant" to ancient customs. The origins of the American concept of judicial review, they contend, must be found elsewhere. This criticism aside, McIlwain's high court theory was a timely antidote to the Whig anachronism of describing medieval parliaments as "absolutely identical" with the legislature of Victoria.

In differentiating between medieval and modern ideas of law making, McIlwain

did not intend to exclude politics and taxation from the agendas of early parliaments, and in later works he reemphasized
these activities. What must be asked is
whether contemporaries considered the
discussion of politics and the granting of
taxes normal functions of medieval parliaments? H. G. Richardson and G. O. Sayles
(selection number four), after four decades of research and publication on the
subject, continue to maintain that meetings of king, council, magnates, and prelates in the thirteenth century (the *afforced*
meetings of the king's council) were not
thought of as parliaments unless there was
judicial activity. The essential, defining
characteristic of parliament was the administration of justice, and all else could
be stripped away as non-essential. In the
reigns of Henry III and Edward I, "representation, legislation, and taxation may be
added . . . but they may be and not infrequently are found in other meetings
which are not parliaments." According to
these authors, then, parliament functioned
as a superior court, where the king, assisted by his judges, lawyers, and clerks,
handled questions from other courts or
dealt with petitions from the country at
large.

The Richardson-Sayles interpretation,
though supported by a wealth of evidence,
has not satisfied contemporary historians
that Stubbs was wrong. R. F. Treharne
studied the use of the word "parliament"
on forty-eight occasions in the mid-thir-
teenth century and concluded that "Englishmen thought of 'parliament' as a primarily political assembly. . . ." [2] Bertie
Wilkinson (selection number five) carried
the case for politics much farther, arguing
that parliament originated as a separate
political assembly outside the king's council, to which were summoned barons and
representatives to "treat" with the king on
great affairs of state. Sir J. G. Edwards,
meanwhile (selection number six),

adopted a middle position, describing
parliament as capable of both judicial and
political business, and adducing evidence
to show that the crown itself considered
parliament a multi-purpose assembly.
Neither function could be arbitrarily
"stripped away" as "non-essential."

If judicial and political activities merited
equal attention in early parliaments, in
what way were these gatherings different
from great councils or colloquies? It may
be that questions about "characteristic"
parliamentary functions have been inap-
propriate, creating differences between
parliaments and other meetings which did
not exist for contemporaries, or at least
did not exist in the degree historians have
assumed.

Yet it was "parliament" and not another
term which eventually came to describe a
specific assembly; crucial to the evolving
nature of that assembly were the summons
to representatives of the counties and boroughs issued in the second half of the
thirteenth century. Edward I, though not
the first king to summon representatives,
was by far the most important figure in
the early stages of parliamentary representation, for during his long reign the
knights and burgesses, after occasional ap-
pearances in the parliaments of Henry III
and Simon de Montfort, became acknowledged members of an emerging institution. The representatives, to be sure,
did not attend all of Edward's parliaments,
but they did attend with increasing frequency and with growing effect. Part II
of this booklet will examine the motives
of Edward I in calling representatives and
consider the degree of their participation
in parliamentary business.

As in so many aspects of the problem
of early parliaments, the answers to this
question of participation differ more in
degree than in kind. Again, points of departure are Stubbs, who stressed the activity of early representatives in areas of
finance, legislation, and general policy,
and Maitland, who saw the 1305 representatives as passive participants concerned

[2] R. F. Treharne, "The Nature of Parliament in
the Reign of Henry III," *English Historical Review,* LXXIV (1959), 610.

mainly with petitioning the crown for favors.

Stubbs's attitude was conditioned by his premise that representation in England developed out of an Anglo-Saxon urge to self-government which a benevolent king recognized and allowed full expression. Edward I "saw what was best for his age and people; he led the way and kept faith." This sympathetic portrayal of Edward as the patriot king has not appealed to twentieth-century historians. Désiré Pasquet (selection number eight) accused Edward of aiming not at self-government but at absolute rule, imposing the onerous duty of representation upon knights and burgesses so that he might break the feudal structure and force everyone into the status of subjects rather than vassals. Or, as T. F. Tout put it, representation was "the shrewd device of an autocrat anxious to use the mass of the people as a check upon his hereditary foes among the greater baronage."[3]

Edward's reputation as an enlightened national leader has never fully recovered from these attacks, but recent writers have dropped the charge of incipient tyranny and tried to understand the king in the context of the feudal society of his day. Edward would be puzzled to hear himself described as anti-feudal; he used the system when it helped him and bypassed or supplemented it when it proved inadequate. At times he was more ruthless than his baronial contemporaries, but on the whole his policies fostered a growing national consciousness and enlarged the "community of the realm."[4]

His most urgent requirement, it now appears, was money, and as the research of May McKisack, J. F. Willard, and S. K.

Mitchell has abundantly shown, representatives were originally summoned for purposes of taxation. Modern investigation has thus underlined the point made long ago by Stubbs. Carl Stephenson (selection number ten) looked at European and English examples of representation before reaching the conclusion that "the principal purpose . . . was to obtain money. . . ." Stephenson found it difficult to believe that Edward, with his pressing financial needs, would have troubled to summon knights and burgesses "merely to facilitate the presentation of petitions."

It is important to ask, here, what role did the representatives play in the tax-granting procedure? Did they possess the political power to withhold taxes as well as grant them, or were they convened merely to secure a favorable public reception of the king's program? Was Edward acting "constitutionally" by placing tax proposals before representatives, or was he observing "due process of law" in order to gain automatic authorization for his demands?

Some answers to these questions can be gotten from an analysis of the writs summoning representatives to parliaments. In these writs, Edward required that the knights and burgesses have "full power" (*plena potestas*) to bind their constituents, so that "business shall not remain unfinished in any way for defect of this power." Sir J. G. Edwards (selection number eleven), as Stubbs before him, interpreted the *plena potestas* to mean that parliamentary representatives exercized a real power of political consent to the royal tax demands. More than this, it "provided the ground work of ideas for that doctrine of parliamentary sovereignty which became . . . 'the dominant characteristic of English political institutions.'"

Gaines Post (selection number thirteen) adopted a contrary view. Tracing the formulas *plena potestas* and *quod omnes tangit ab omnibus approbetur* (what concerns all should be approved by

[3] T. F. Tout, Chapters in the *Administrative History of Medieval England,* 6 volumes (Manchester, 1920–1933), II, 190.
[4] See especially, R. S. Hoyt, "Royal Demesne, Parliamentary Taxation, and the Realm, 1294–1322," *Speculum,* XXIII (1948), 58–69, and M. R. Powicke, "The General Obligation to Cavalry Service Under Edward I," *Speculum,* XXVIII (1953), 814–833.

all) to their Roman and canon law sources, he illustrated the overriding legal characteristics of the phrases, arguing that they signified "in ordinary judicial procedure . . . the litigants' full acceptance of, or consent to, the court's decision of the case." When applied to parliaments, the Romano-canonical formulas strengthened the king, enabling him on the basis of political necessity and royal prerogative to obtain in advance the representatives' consent to the "decisions" of king and council. If consent to crown demands was, as Post suggested, "judicial-conciliar," and not political, Edward I's parliament assumes more the character of Maitland's royal court than of Stubbs's representative assembly.

Post's application of Roman and canon law formulas to medieval parliaments raises the question to be considered in Part III, to what extent did the process of representation originate in England and to what extent was it adapted from European example? Needless to say, the school of "national" historians of the Victorian age emphasized the uniqueness of the English parliamentary experience; no other conclusion seemed warranted at the time, in view of the triumph of parliament over the Stuarts in 1688 and the corresponding failure of representative assemblies everywhere in Europe. But historians today have taken a closer look at European representative institutions and found their medieval history as varied and complex as that of the English parliament.[5] The vigorous existence of the Spanish Cortes, the French States General, and other European assemblies seemed to A. R. Myers (selection number fifteen) sufficient rebuttal of the commonplace English belief that these assemblies were "rare, transient, narrow in basis or weak in

power," and to C. H. McIlwain, "sufficient answer to any theory of their exclusively 'Anglo-Saxon' origin and character." [6] English parliaments, instead of being viewed as prototypes, were now considered part of an institutional development common to Europe in the twelfth and thirteenth centuries. The place of origin could well be Spain, southern France, Italy, or England.

What caused the spread, or "diffusion" of representative institutions across medieval Europe? According to Sir Ernest Barker, the Dominican Order was responsible both for developing representation and carrying the practice to England by way of southern France, the meeting ground of St. Dominic and the elder Simon de Montfort. The evidence for and against Barker's thesis is evaluated by H. P. Tunmore (selection number twelve). Gaines Post, as we have seen, considered Roman and canon law to be the vehicle for the spread of ideas of representation and consent, while others have explained the process in the common needs and ambitions of medieval kings. "It may be suggested . . . ," wrote J. R. Strayer, "that one of the chief reasons for the growth of parliamentary institutions in thirteenth-century Europe was that lay rulers found it necessary to secure publicity for their acts." [7] And what better agents of publicity, Helen Cam proposed (selection number nine), than local representatives awed by the spectacle of the royal court? Waging war was another activity common to medieval monarchs, and here again, representative practice seems to have been advanced through military assemblies convoked by a regular pattern of summons. This explanation, T. N. Bisson observed, has been little noticed by historians, possibly because of the modern assumption that militarism and representation are in-

[5] See, for example, the series, *Studies Presented to the International Commission for the History of Representative and Parliamentary Institutions,* 28 volumes to date (Louvain and other cities, 1937–1965). Among the authors contributing are E. Lousse, A. Marongiu, H. G. Richardson, G. O. Sayles, F. L. Carsten, and J. Russell Major.

[6] C. H. McIlwain, "Medieval Estates," *Cambridge Medieval History* (1932), VII, 682.
[7] J. R. Strayer, "The Statute of York and the Community of the Realm," *American Historical Review,* XLVII (1941), 5.

compatible, a premise generally true in the twentieth century but scarcely applicable to the Middle Ages, when "those who ruled were still mainly those who fought." [8]

If the English parliament was not unique among medieval representative institutions it nevertheless had distinguishing characteristics. Helen Cam (selection number fourteen) considered it "absolutely exceptional," basing her conclusion on the fact that in England, unlike Europe, representation developed first on the local level where there was no corporate tradition or Roman law influence, and was later transferred to the national level by Angevin administrative reforms. Cam's interpretation combines the "traditional formulas" of Stubbs with A. B. White's theory of self-government "at the king's command" and produces anew a pattern of development in England different from that on the Continent. Parliamentary representation was not something added to the "community of the realm"; it was drawn out of the "community of the vill."

It has been the aim of this booklet to show that England's parliament has "no one origin, nor can it be comprehended in any simple formula of growth." [9] Certainly these few pages cannot give a clear answer to questions about the origins of parliament or of representation; even the documents hold only a portion of that answer, with the rest lost in what Sir Maurice Powicke has described as "the mystery which attends on all beginnings. . . ." Far from dispelling the "mystery" of parliamentary beginnings, the selections, with their subtle shadings of interpretation, illustrate the limits of the most careful research, and show us the inadequacy of easy generalizations about medieval institutions. For if we are to understand the Middle Ages at all, we must remember the warning of Maitland: "as we go backwards the familiar outlines become blurred; the ideas become fluid, and instead of the simple we find the indefinite."

[8] T. N. Bisson, "The Military Origins of Medieval Representation," *American Historical Review,* LXXI (1966), 1199, 1213, 1218.

[9] J. E. A. Joliffe, "Some Factors in the Beginnings of Parliament," *Transactions of the Royal Historical Society,* 4th Series, XXII (1940), 139. [NOTE: Footnotes have generally been omitted except where needed to explain text.]

# GLOSSARY

Listed below are brief definitions of selected technical terms and statutes mentioned in the readings.

**BRACTON**   Henrici de Bracton (1210–1268), Dean of Exeter, king's clerk, justice in eyre, justice of the King's Bench, and author of *Tractatus de Legibus et Consuetudinebus Angliae* (*A Treatise about the Laws and Customs of England*).

**COMMON LAW**   "Common law is . . . unenacted law. . . . common to the whole land. . . . the law of the temporal courts. . . . Common law is in theory traditional law—that which has always been law and still is law, in so far as it has not been overridden by statute or ordinance. . . . More and more common law is gradually evolved as ever new cases arise; but the judges are not conceived as making new law . . . rather they are but declaring what has always been law." (F. W. Maitland)

**CONFIRMATION OF THE CHARTERS, 1297**   Document which confirmed Magna Carta and the Forest Charters, and more importantly, committed the king not to levy "aids, taxes, and prises, except by the common assent of the whole kingdom and for the common benefit of the same kingdom, saving the ancient aids and prises due and accustomed." Historians are in disagreement concerning the meaning of this phrase.

**FLETA**   A commentary on English law written during the reign of Edward I, probably by one of the king's ex-judges, then in the Fleet Prison.

**HILARYTIDE**   See LEGAL TERM DAYS.

**LEGAL TERM DAYS**   The periods in which litigation was permitted by the Church were named for the feast days preceding their beginnings: Hilarytide (St. Hilary, January 13), Easter (movable), Holy Trinity (movable), and Michaelmas (St. Michael, September 29). Historians have noted an intimate connection between meetings of parliaments and legal terms.

**MATTHEW PARIS**   Medieval chronicler (d. 1259).

**MICHAELMAS**   See LEGAL TERM DAYS.

**ORDAINERS**   See ORDINANCES OF 1311.

**ORDINANCES OF 1311**   Document issued by a baronial commission of twenty-one, the Lords Ordainers, which described the governmental reforms forced upon Edward II.

**PERCENTAGE TAXES**   Taxes on personal property assessed in parliamentary assemblies became a major source of royal revenue in the last decade of the thirteenth century. They usually took the form of a double rate, for example, an "eighth" and "twelfth," with the burgesses paying a higher rate than landowners because their liquid assets were more easily concealed from tax agents. Taxes in this period ranged from the sixth and tenth of 1294 to the twentieth and thirtieth of 1306.

*Placita*   Suits of court.

*Plena Potestas*   A phrase in parliamentary writs of summons which required knights and burgesses to have "full powers" to act for their constituents, "so that, through default of such authority . . . business shall by no means remain unfinished."

Provisions of Oxford   Document establishing a baronial committee of twenty-four to reform Henry III's government in 1258. Among the provisions was a clause requiring three parliaments a year, to which shall come the "chosen councillors of the king" and "twelve good men" of the community, "to consider the affairs of the king and kingdom."

Provisions of Westminster   Drawn up at the Westminster parliament of 1259, this document released subtenants and mesne tenants from the duty of responding to their overlords' suits of court. The Statute of Marlborough, 1267, incorporated this idea.

*Quia Emptores*   See Statute of Westminster III.

*Quo Warranto*   Inquest conducted by Edward I in 1274–1275 to determine by what authority — *quo warranto* — his barons exercised their feudal rights and franchises. *Quo Warranto* procedures were explained in the Statute to Gloucester (1278) and the Statute of *Quo Warranto* (1290).

*Quod Omnes Tangit (ab omnibus approbetur)*   A phrase in the preamble to the writs of summons to the clergy in 1295 which declares, "what concerns all should be approved by all." Historians disagree over its constitutional significance.

Rolls of Parliament   The enrolled records of parliaments begin in the reign of Edward I, but there is no systematic recording until the reign of Edward III. The House of Lords ordered published all rolls then known in 1767, under the title *Rotuli Parliamentorum*. For the rolls of parliament edited and published since that time, see the "Suggested Readings" at the end of this booklet.

Rolls Series   Shortened title of *Rerum Brittanicarum Medii Aevi Scriptores,* or *Chronicles and Memorials of Great Britain and Ireland During the Middle Ages,* 254 volumes (London, 1858–1911). Among the editors were William Stubbs, F. W. Maitland, L. O. Pike, and J. Gairdner.

SIMON DE MONTFORT  Leader of the baronial reform movement who came to power by defeating Henry III at the Battle of Lewes in 1264, and then summoned knights and burgesses to a parliament. In August, 1265, he was defeated and killed by Prince Edward at the Battle of Evesham.

STATUTE OF MARLBOROUGH  See PROVISIONS OF WESTMINSTER.

STATUTE OF WESTMINSTER II ·(*De Donis Conditionalibus*, 1285)  The statute "concerning conditional gifts" forbade land owners to break up their estates. It led to the practice of entail and the preservation of large landed estates in England.

STATUTE OF WESTMINSTER III (*Quia Emptores*, 1290)  Was designed to check subinfeudation by prohibiting any land transfers which created sub-vassals or mesne tenants. In the transfer of land, the seller relinquished all his feudal rights and the buyer incurred obligations only to the original owner of the land.

STATUTES AND ORDINANCES  Two methods of promulgating law in medieval England, which down to the reign of Edward III were similar in their legal effect. Usually, statutes were issued in parliament and ordinances in a session of the king's council.

STATUTES OF THE REALM  The recording of English laws became a conscious policy in the reign of Edward I, when the flood of legislation made necessary the Statute Rolls. Statutes are listed according to their order in each monarch's regnal year: 3 Edward I, *capitulum* [law, or heading] 5.

TALLAGE  Tax levied by the crown upon towns and lands in the royal demesne.

# The Conflict of Opinion

Was parliament in the thirteenth century a "national assembly of the three estates," or was it a "session of the king's council"?

"To this point then had the parliamentary constitution grown under the hand of this great king..The assembly definitely constituted in 1295, — at once a representation of the three estates and a concentration of the local institutions, — the clergy, the barons and the communities, associated for financial, legislative, and political action — obtained in 1297 the fullest recognition of its rights as representing the whole nation."
— WILLIAM STUBBS

". . . a session of the king's council is the core and essence of every *parliamentum* . . . the documents usually called 'parliamentary petitions' are petitions to the king and his council . . . the auditors of petitions are committees of the council . . . the rolls of parliament are the records of the business done by the council — sometimes with, but much more often without, the concurrence of the estates of the realm — . . . the highest tribunal in England is not a general assembly of barons and prelates, but the king's council. . . ."
— F. W. MAITLAND

In function, was it concerned essentially with the "administration of justice," or was it "omnicompetent," and interested in all matters of lay government?

"We believe . . . 'that parliaments are of one kind only and that . . . the essence of them is the dispensing of justice.'"
— H. G. RICHARDSON AND G. O. SAYLES

"Important 'judicial' functions could be, and often were, performed in parliament, but the essence of its functions was not specifically judicial, any more than it was specifically legislative, or specifically taxative, or specifically anything. The essence of its function consisted in being *unspecific*, in being omnicompetent . . ."
— SIR J. G. EDWARDS

What motivated Edward I to enlarge the practice of representation begun by his predecessors? Was he aiming for absolute power, publicizing controversial programs, or bolstering faltering finances?

"Despite its feudal form, the summoning of the commons was an essentially anti-feudal measure, the object of which was to . . . subject all the inhabitants of the realm, of whatever rank in the feudal hierarchy, to the direct authority of the monarch."
— DÉSIRÉ PASQUET

"In 1283 and again in 1295 and 1307 Edward I was undoubtedly, like his contemporary Phillippe le Bel, making use of the representative system for propaganda purposes. . . ."

— HELEN CAM

"Although the king might use communal delegates in a variety of ways, the compelling motive behind their incorporation as an estate of parliament was economic."

— CARL STEPHENSON

Were representative parliaments uniquely English in their origins, or were they part of a general thirteenth century European phenomenon?

"And so we may urge that the Church by its organization, its ideas, its procedure, was a model and a precedent for that parliamentary system, which, we must admit and indeed urge, in turn reacted on the Church. . . ." [THE DOMINICAN ORDER AND CONVOCATION (1913), p. 74.]

— SIR ERNEST BARKER

"Of all the terminology taken from the Roman law and accepted throughout western Europe by the middle of the thirteenth century, *plena potestas* was one of the most significant expressions of the new relationship between the communities and the central authority."

— GAINES POST

"It is the survival of the shire that is unique; and it is the shire that makes the English parliament absolutely exceptional."

— HELEN CAM

". . . in its numerous representative institutions the countries of Latin Christendom . . . created something unique to Western Civilization. . . ."

— A. R. MYERS

# I. THE BUSINESS OF EARLY ENGLISH PARLIAMENTS: HIGH POLITICS OR THE ADMINISTRATION OF JUSTICE?

## The National Assembly of the Three Estates

### WILLIAM STUBBS

William Stubbs (1825–1901), Regius Professor of Modern History at Oxford, Bishop of Chester, and Bishop of Oxford, was the founder of modern historiography in England. Through his own indefatigable example (he edited nineteen volumes for the Rolls Series in a twenty-five year period) Stubbs set the pattern of writing history from documents, rather than from secondary sources. Of his work, F. W. Maitland wrote, "no other Englishman has so completely displayed to the world the whole business of the historian from the winning of the raw material to the narrating and generalising." Stubbs' three-volume *Constitutional History of England* (1874–1878) immediately became the standard work in its field, and though many of its interpretations have been revised, it still ranks as a basic secondary source. In the selection below, taken from the *Constitutional History*, Stubbs describes the English parliament as a national assembly of the three estates, convened for purposes of taxation, legislation, and deliberation.

W<small>E HAVE</small> in former chapters examined the powers of the national council under the Norman and Plantagenet kings, and in the last chapter have watched the constant attempts made by personal and political parties to extend them. We have seen too how those attempts coincide in time with an irregular but continuous enlargement of the constitution of the national council. The next question is to determine how far and by what degrees the new elements of parliament were admitted to an equal share with the older elements in the powers which were already obtained or asserted; how far and by what steps were the commons placed on a constitutional level with the other two estates during the period of definition.

The great council of the nation, before the end of the reign of John, had obtained the acknowledgment and enjoyed the exercise of the following rights. In respect of taxation, the theoretical assent, which under the Norman kings had been taken for granted, had been exchanged for a real consultation; the *commune concilium*[1] had first discussed the finance of the year under Henry II, had next demurred to the nature

[1] Confronted with this phrase and the similar *commune consilium*, Stubbs thought the first (*concilium*) described a pre-parliamentary assembly and the second (*consilium*) implied the act of consulting. A. B. White, "Was There a 'Common Council' Before Parliament," *American Historical Review*, XXV (1919), 1—17, argues that spelled either way, the phrase meant only the act of common consultation. [Editor's note.]

From William Stubbs, *The Constitutional History of England*, 4th edition, 3 volumes (London, 1896), II, pp. 248–268, 273–278.

1

of the exaction under Richard, and under John had obtained in the Great Charter the concession that without their consent given in a duly convoked assembly no tax should be levied beyond the three prescriptive feudal aids. They had further, by the practice of the king's ministers in the exchequer, been consulted as to the mode of assessment, and had given counsel and consent to the form in which the taxes were collected. In respect of legislation they had received similar formal recognition of their right to advise and consent, and had, as it would appear from the preamble of some of the assizes, exercised a power of initiating amendments of the law by means of petition. As a high court of justice they had heard the complaints of the king against individuals, and had accepted and ratified his judgments against high offenders. And lastly as a supreme deliberative council they had been consulted on questions of foreign policy, of internal police and national defence; in the absence of the king from England they had practically exercised the right of regulating the regency, at all events in the case of the deposition of Longchamp; and by a series of acts of election, acknowledgment, and acceptance of the kings at their accession, had obtained a recognition of their right to regulate the succession also.

During the minority and in the troubled years of Henry III they had fully vindicated and practically enlarged these rights. In matters of taxation they had frequently refused aid to the king, and when they granted it they had carefully prescribed the mode of collection and assessment; in legislation they had not only taken the initiative by petitions, such as those which led to the Provisions of Oxford, and by articles of complaint presented by the whole or a portion of their body, but they had, as in the famous act of the council of Merton touching the legitimising of bastards by the subsequent marriage of their parents, refused their consent to a change in the law, by words which were accepted by the jurists as the statement of a con-

stitutional fact. Their judicial power was abridged in practice by the strengthened organisation of the royal courts, but it remained in full force in reference to high offenders, and causes between great men; the growth of the privileges of baronage gave to the national council, as an assembly of barons, the character of a court of peers for the trial and amercement of their fellows; and, even where a cause was brought against the king himself, although it must begin with a petition of right and not as in causes between subjects with a writ, the lawyers recognised the *universitas regni* [*whole realm*] as the source of remedy, and the king's court as one of the three powers which are above the king himself. Their general political power was greatly increased; they had determined the policy of the crown in foreign affairs; they had not only displaced the king's ministers but had placed the royal power itself in commission; they had drawn up a new constitution for the country and imposed new oaths on the king and his heir. It is true that the most important of these were party measures, carried out in exceptional times and by unconstitutional means, but it was as representing the supreme council of the kingdom that the baronial party acted, and the rights they enforced were enforced in the name of the nation.

But the claims of the same body had gone further, and had in some respects run far in advance of the success which was actually achieved at the time or for ages later; nay, in one or two points they had claimed powers which have never yet been formally conceded. The principles that the grant of money should depend on the redress of grievances, and that the parliament should determine the destination of a grant by making conditions as to expenditure, were admitted by the royal advisers, although the king contrived to evade the concession. The right of electing the ministers, a premature and imperfect realisation of the doctrine of a limited monarchy, was likewise demanded as authorised by ancient practice. The right of controlling the king's action by a resident elective council also was asserted; but, though Henry was constrained to accept these terms, he steadily refused to admit them as a matter of right, and they were ultimately rejected with the acquiescence of the nation.

The early years of Edward I saw all the privileges which had been really used or acquired under Henry III fully exercised. The parliament of prelates and barons had been asked for and had granted aids, had given counsel and consent to legislation, had acted as a supreme court of justice, and had discussed questions of foreign policy and internal administration. The further steps gained by the constitutional assembly in this reign were gained by it in its new and complete organisation.

Two drawbacks materially affected the value of these rights: the recognition of certain power on the king's part to do by his own authority acts of the same class as those for which he asked counsel and consent; and the recognition of certain undefined rights of individual members to concede or refuse consent to the determinations of the whole body; the latter drawback was seriously increased by the incompleteness of the national representation before the 23rd of Edward I.

Although the national council had made out its right to be heard on all four points of administrative policy, it had not obtained an exclusive right to determine that policy. The taxes might be granted in parliament, but the king could still take the customary aids without reference to parliament; he could tallage his demesnes and could interpret the title of demesne so as to bring the chartered towns, or a large portion of them, under contribution; he could increase the customs by separate negotiations with the merchants, and at any time raise money by gifts negotiated with individual payers, and assessed by the officers of the exchequer. The laws again were issued with counsel and consent of the parliament, but legal enactments might, as before, in the shape of assizes or ordinances, be issued

without any such assistance; and the theory of the enacting power of the king, as supreme legislator, grew rather than diminished during the period, probably in consequence of the legislative activity of Frederick II, Lewis IX, and Alfonso the Wise. The king's court, the curia regis, might be influenced and used to defeat the right of the barons to be judged by their peers, and there was not in the article of the charter anything that so fixed the method of such judgment as to make it necessary to transact it in full council. And the political action of the crown, in matters both foreign and domestic, could, as it always can, be determined without reference to anything but the royal will. Nor, as we shall see, was the failure of the national council to secure exclusive enjoyment of these rights owing to their own weakness: both Henry III and Edward I possessed, in their personal inner council, a body of advisers organised so as to maintain the royal authority on these points, a council by whose advice they acted, judged, legislated, and taxed when they could, and the abuse of which was not yet prevented by any constitutional check. The opposition between the royal and the national councils, between the privy council and the parliament, is an important element in later national history.

The second, however, of these points, the uncertainty of the line dividing corporate and individual consent, and the consequent difficulty of adjusting national action with incomplete representation, bears more directly on the subject before us. The first question has already arisen: did the consent of a baron in council to grant a tax bind him individually only, or did it form part of such a general consent as would be held to bind those who refused consent? When Geoffrey or York, or Ranulf of Chester, refused to agree to a grant, was the refusal final or was it overborne by the consent of the majority? Did the baron who promised aid make a private promise or authorise a general tax? Was taxation the fulfilment of individual voluntary engagements or the legal result of a sovereign act? Secondly, how far could the consent, even if it were unanimous, of a national council composed of barons and superior clergy, bind the unrepresented classes, the commons, and the parochial clergy? The latter question is practically answered by the contrivances used to reconcile compulsion with equity. The writ of Edward I for the collection of the aid *pur fille marier* [for the marriage of his daughter] rehearses that it was granted in full parliament by certain bishops and barons, for themselves and for the community of the whole realm, "so far as in them lay." As a parliamentary assembly, legally summoned, they authorised a tax which would bind all tenants of the crown, but they did it with an express limitation, a conscious hesitation, and the king did not at the time venture to collect the tax. This was on the very eve of the contest for the confirmation of the charters. The documentary history of the reign of Henry III illustrates the difficulty at an earlier stage. In 1224 the prelates granted a carucage[2] of half a mark on their demesne lands and those of their immediate tenants, and two shillings on the lands of the under tenants of those tenants: the feudal lord thus represented all who held directly or mediately under him. In 1232 the writ for collecting the fortieth states that it was granted by the archbishops, bishops, abbots, priors, clergy, earls, barons, knights, freeholders, and villeins, implying that not only the national council but the county courts had been dealt with: but in 1237 a similar writ rehearses the consent of the prelates, barons, knights and freeholders for themselves and their villeins. Yet it is certain that in neither of the parliaments in which these taxes were granted were the villeins represented, and almost as certain that the commons were unrepresented also. The consent thus rehearsed must have been a simple fabrication, a legal fiction, on a theoretical view of parliament; or else the exacting process of the central

assembly must have been supplemented by the consent of the county courts, in which alone, at the time, the liberi homines and villani assembled, that consent being either taken by the itinerant judges or presumed to follow on a proclamation by the sheriff. The expressions, however used, show a misgiving, and warrant the conclusion that the line between corporate and individual, general and local, consent was lightly drawn: the theory that the lord represented his vassal was too dangerous to be unreservedly admitted when all men were the king's vassals; the need of representation was felt. But the line continued uncertain until 1295; and even after that the variety of proportion in which the several estates taxed themselves shows that the distinction between a voluntary gift and an enacted tax was imperfectly realised.

The idea that the refusal of an individual baron to grant the tax absolved him from the necessity of paying it, although now and then broached by a too powerful subject, could be easily overborne by force: ordinarily the king would seize the lands of the contumacious, and take by way of fine or ransom what could not be extracted by way of gift. The claim of a particular community to refuse a tax which had not been assented to by its own representatives, such as was claimed in the sixteenth century by Ghent, was based on the same idea, and would be overcome in the same way. Such a hypothesis, however, could only arise in a community which had not realised the nature of sovereign rights or of national identity. The refusal of an estate of the realm to submit to taxation imposed in an assembly at which it had not been represented, or to which its representatives had not been summoned, rested on a different basis. Such was the plea of the clergy in 1254, and it was recognised by the spirit of the constitution.

The practice had long been to take the consent of the communities by special commission. The year 1295 marks the date at which the special commissions, as a rule, cease, and the communities appear by their

---

[2] Carucage was a tax levied by the crown on one's plough-team, or plough-land. [Editor's note.]

representatives to join in the act of the sovereign body. The process of transition belongs to the years 1282 and 1295, and the transition implies the admission of the commons to a share of taxing power, together with the clergy and the baronage.

The dates may be more precisely marked. In 1282 the king's treasurer negotiated with the several shires and boroughs for a subsidy, just as might have been done under Henry II: the money so collected being insufficient, the king at Rhuddlan summoned the clergy and commons to two provincial councils, in one of which the commons granted a thirtieth on condition that the barons should do the same. In 1289 a special negotiation was proposed, but not carried into effect. In 1290 the barons granted an aid *pur fille marier;* the knights of the shire were subsequently summoned to join in a grant of a fifteenth; and the clergy in a separate assembly voted a tenth of spirituals; the boroughs probably, and the city of London certainly, paid the fifteenth without having been represented in the assembly that voted it, except as parts of the shires represented by the knights. In 1294 the clergy in September granted a moiety of their entire revenue in a parliamentary assembly of the two provinces held at Westminster; the earls, barons, and knights granted a tenth in November, and commissioners were sent out in the same month to request a sixth from the cities and boroughs; the three estates, roughly divided, thus granted their money at different dates, in different proportions, and in different ways. In 1295 the special negotiation disappears: the three estates, although making their grants in different measure and by separate vote, are fully represented, and act in this, as in other respects, in the character of a consolidated parliament.

Nor was the recognition of this right of taxation confined to direct money grants. The impost on wool, woolfells and leather, has a similar history, although the steps of reform are different and the immediate burden fell not on an estate but on in-

dividual merchants. In 1275 we are told that the prelates, magnates, and communities, at the request of the merchants granted a custom on these commodities: in 1294 a large increase of custom was imposed by the king's decree, rehearsing however the consent of the merchants, not that of the parliament. In the articles of 1297 the royal right of taxing wool was placed under the same restrictions as the right of direct taxation; but the idea was still maintained that an increase of the impost might be legalised by the consent of the payers, and an attempt to substitute the action of a "colloquium" of merchants for that of the national parliament was defeated by the representatives of the boroughs in 1303.

The confirmation of charters in 1297 recognised on the king's part the exclusive right of the parliament to authorise taxation: "for no occasion from henceforth will we take such manner of aids, tasks, or prises, but by the common assent of the realm and for the common profit thereof, saving the ancient aids and prises due and accustomed." Already the right of the commons to a share in the taxing power of parliament was admitted.

The right of the three estates to share in legislation was established by a different process and on a different theory; it was a result rather than a cause of the recognition of their character as a supreme council. The consent of individuals was much less important in the enacting or improving of the law than in the levying of a tax; the power of counsel in the one case might fairly be supposed to belong to one of the three estates in larger proportion than to the others; and the enacting, if not also the initiative, power belonged to the king. The nation granted the tax, the king enacted the law: the nation might consent to the tax in various ways, severally by estates, communities, or individuals, or corporately in parliament; but the law was enacted once for all by the king with the advice and consent of parliament; it was no longer in the power of the individual, the community, or the estate to withhold its obedience with impunity. In very early times it is possible that the local assemblies were required to give assent to the legal changes made by the central authority, that a publication of the new law in the shire-moot was regarded as denoting the acceptance of it by the people in general, and that it would be contrary to natural equity to enforce a law which had not been so published. But from the existing remains of legislation, we are forced to conclude that, whilst customary law was recorded in the memories of the people, legislative action belonged only to the wise, that is to the royal or national council. That council in the twelfth century contained only the magnates; at the end of the thirteenth it contained also the inferior clergy and the commons: the latter, fully competent as they were to discuss a tax, were not equally competent to frame a law; and such right of initiation as the right of petition involved could be set in motion outside as easily as inside parliament. Yet the right of the nation to determine by what laws it would be governed was fully admitted. Canute and the Conqueror had heard the people accept and swear to the laws of Edgar and Edward. The Great Charter and the Provisions of Oxford were promulgated in the county courts, and all men were bound by oath to obey them, as if without such acceptance they lacked somewhat of legal force. Bracton, in the words of Justinian, enumerates the "consensus utentium" [consent of the users] as well as the king's oath among the bases of law. It is to the conservation of the laws which the folk, vulgus, communaulté, shall have chosen, that the later coronation oath binds the king. The enactment of Edward II in 1322, that matters to be established touching the estate of the king and his heirs, the realm and the people, shall be treated, accorded, and established in parliaments by the king and by the assent of the prelates, earls, and barons and the commonalty of the realm, is but an amplification of the principle laid down by his father in 1295.

The legislation, however, of the reign of Henry III, and most of that of Edward I, was the work of assemblies to which the commons were not summoned. It has been well remarked that, whereas for his political work Edward found himself obliged to obtain the co-operation of the three estates, his legislative work was done without the co-operation of the commons, until in the question of taxation they had enforced their right to be heard. By whatever process the consent of the "communaulté" to the statute of Westminster the first was signified, and whatever were the force of the summons by virtue of which the "communaulté" was supposed to be present, it is certain that in 1290 the statute "quia emptores" was passed in a council at which no representatives of the commons attended, and as certain that the statute of Carlisle was published after deliberation not only with the magnates but with the "communitates" of the realm. The statute "quia emptores" was not improbably the last case in which the assent of the commons was taken for granted in legislation: for in the later enactments by ordinance it is not the commons only but the parliament itself that is set aside; and, although some few statutes made after 1290 do not declare expressly the participation of the three estates, it is possible, by comparing the dates of those acts with the extant writs of summons, to show that all such acts as were really laws were enacted in full parliaments to which the words of the statute of Carlisle are equally applicable. The commons had now a share of the "commune consilium regni" which was indispensable to the abrogation or amendment of a law. It is true that some of the most important acts of parliament are dated several days after the writs were issued for the payment of the wages of the knights and burghers, e.g. in 1300 the Articuli Super Cartas are published April 15, the writs for wages are issued March 20; in 1301 the letters to the pope are dated February 12; the writs, January 30. Not much however can be argued from this, for the final form which the law took would be settled at the end of the parliament; the representatives might leave as soon as the important business of petition and consultation was over. There could be no reason why they should stay until the charters were actually sealed or the copies of the statutes written out for circulation.

But neither this conclusion nor even the principle stated by Edward II in 1322, implies the absolute equality of the share of each estate. Counsel and consent are ascribed to the magnates, but it is a long time before more is allowed generally to the commons than petition, instance, or request: and the right of petition the commons possessed even when not called together to parliament; the community of a county might declare a grievance, just as the grand jury presented a criminal. Further, so long as the enacting power was exercised by the king, with the counsel and consent of the magnates only, a statute might be founded on a petition of the clergy; and it may be questioned whether, according to the legal idea of Edward I, an act so initiated and authorised would not be a law without consent of the commons, just as an act framed on the petition of the commons would, if agreed to by the magnates, become law without consent of the clergy either in convocation or in parliament. The determination of this point belongs to the history of the following century. We conclude that, for the period before us, it would be true to say, that, although in theory legislation was the work of the king in full parliament, he exercised the power of legislating without a full parliament, and that in the full parliament itself the functions of the three estates were in this respect imperfectly defined. It is certain however, from the action of the king in reference to mortmain, that a statute passed with the counsel and consent of parliament, however constituted, could not be abrogated without the same counsel and consent.

The third attribute of the old national council, that of a supreme tribunal of justice, for the trial of great offenders, and the determination of great causes, was never shared by the commons. The nearest approach to such a participation was made when in 1283 they were summoned to Shrewsbury, on the trial of David of Wales: but they attended merely as witnesses of the trial; he was tried by the king's judges and only in the presence, not by a tribunal, of his peers. It is true that the abundant facilities which the system of jury gave for the trial of commoners by their peers superseded any necessity for criminal jurisdiction to be exercised by the assembly of the commons; but it is not quite so clear why the right of advising the crown in the determination of civil cases was restricted to the lords, or why they should continue to form a council for the hearing of petitions to the king, when the commons did not join in their deliberations. This resulted however from the fact that the system of petition to the king in council had been perfected before the commons were called to parliament; and thus the whole subject of judicature belongs to the history of the royal council rather than to that of parliament strictly so called. But it is noteworthy in connexion with the fact that the estate which retained the judicial power of the national council retained also the special right of counsel and consent in legislation, these rights being a survival of the time when the magnates were the whole parliament; and on the other hand the smaller council which, as the king's special advisers, exercised judicial authority in Chancery, or in Privy Council and Star-chamber, claimed also the right of legislating by ordinance.

The general deliberative functions of parliament, and the right of the representatives of the commons to share with the magnates in discussing foreign affairs or internal administration, scarcely come before us during this period with sufficient distinctness to enable us to mark any steps of progress. On the other hand the right of deliberation had been exercised by the great men long before the time of the Great Charter, and abundant evidence shows that they retained the right. The stories of the debate on the "Quo Warranto" and the action of the earls in 1297 fully illustrate this. The action of the commons is distinctly traceable in the presentation of the Bill of twelve articles at the parliament of Lincoln in 1301. That bill was a bill of the prelates and proceres delivered on behalf of the whole community, but presented by a knight of the shire for Lancashire. The representatives of the commons had left before the barons drew up their letter to the pope. Here again it is probable that the theory of the constitution was somewhat in advance of its actual progress. The principle declared by Edward I in 1295 would seem to touch this function of the national council more directly even than taxation or legislation; but in practice, as had been done long ago, silence was construed as assent and counsel taken for granted from the absent as well as the present.

The forms of the writs of summons furnish illustrations if not conclusive evidence on the general question. The special writs addressed to the magnates usually define their function in council by the word *tractare* [to treat]. In 1205 the bishop of Salisbury is summoned to treat on the common interest of the realm; in 1241 the bishops and barons are summoned *ad tractandum* [to treat]; in 1253 to hear the king's pleasure and to treat with his council; in Simon de Montfort's writ for 1265 the words are *tractaturi et consilium vestrum impensuri* [to consider the matters set forth and to give your counsel regarding them]; to the first parliament of Edward I the archbishop of Canterbury is invited *ad tractandum et ordinandum* [to treat and to ordain]; to the parliament of Shrewsbury in 1283 the barons are summoned *nobiscum locuturi* [to speak with us]; in 1294 the king declares his wish to hold *colloquium et tractatum* [a conference and a consideration]; in 1295 earls, barons,

and prelates are summoned *ad tractandum, ordinandum et faciendum nobiscum et cum praelatis et ceteris proceribus et aliis incolis regni nostri* [to treat, ordain and do, along with us and with the rest of the prelates and principal men and other inhabitants of our kingdom]; in 1297 the barons only, *colloquium et tractatum specialiter habituri vestrumque consilium impensuri* [to have a particular conference and a consideration and to give your counsel]; in 1298 the form is *tractatum et colloquium habituri* [to treat and to have a conference]; and from 1299 generally *tractaturi vestrumque consilium impensuri* [to treat and to give your counsel]. In this last formula we have the fullest statement of the powers which, on Edward's theory of government, were exercised by those constituents of the national council that had for the longest time been summoned: and these functions must be understood as being shared by the judges and other councillors who are summoned in almost exactly the same terms.

The writs ordering the return of representative knights run as follows; in 1213 John summons them *ad loquendum nobiscum de negotiis regni nostri* [to speak with us concerning the affairs of our kingdom]; in 1254 the special purpose is expressed *ad providendum . . . quale auxilium . . . impendere velint* [to see . . . what sort of aid . . . they might wish to give us]; in 1261 the words are *colloquium habituros* [to have a conference]; in 1264 *nobiscum tractaturi* [to treat with us]; under Simon de Montfort in 1265 all the representatives are summoned in the same form as the magnates; in 1275 the form is *ad tractandum* [to treat]; in 1282 the character of the full power which they receive from their constituencies is expressed, *ad audiendum et faciendum ea quae sibi ex parte nostra faciemus ostendi* [to hear and to do those things which, on our side, we will make known to them]: in 1283 the words are *super hiis et aliis locuturi* [to speak concerning these and other affairs]: in 1290 the full powers are described, *ad consulendum et consentiendum pro se et communitate illa hiis quae comites, barones et proceres praedicti tunc duxerint concordanda* [to counsel and consent, for themselves and for that community, to those things which the earls, barons and magnates aforesaid then shall have brought forward to be agreed upon]; in 1294 *ad consulendum et consentiendum* [to counsel and consent]; in 1295 both knights of the shire and representatives of the towns are to be chosen *ad faciendum quod tunc de communi consilio ordinabitur* [to do what shall then be ordained by common counsel]; and this form is retained until under Edward II the words *ad consentiendum* [to consent] are added.

The variations of expression may safely be interpreted as showing some uncertainty as to the functions of the representatives, although, as in the case of the barons, it may often merely show the difference of the occasion for which they were summoned. But it would be wrong to infer from the words in which their full representative powers were described that their functions were ever limited to mere consent to the resolutions of the magnates. Certainly this was not the case in questions of taxation, in which the several bodies deliberated and determined apart. The fact that the representative or delegate powers are so carefully described in the later writs shows the care taken, at the time of transition from taxation by local consent to taxation by general enactment, that no community should escape contribution by alleging the incompleteness of the powers with which it had invested its delegates; *ita quod pro defectu hujus potestatis negotium praedictum infectum non remaneat quoquo modo* [so that the aforesaid business shall not remain unfinished in any way for defect of this power]. The delegates had full procuratorial power both to advise and to execute. The fact however remains that, although the assembly was called for advice and co-operation, it was co-operation rather than advice that was expected from the commons: counsel is

distinctly mentioned in the invitation to the magnates, action and consent in the invitation to representatives. Similar variations are to be found in the writs directing the parliamentary representation of the clergy; in 1295 the proctors as well as the prelates are summoned *ad tractandum, ordinandum et faciendum* [to treat, ordain and do]; in 1299 the form is *ad faciendum et consentiendum* [to do and consent]. Under Edward III *faciendum* is frequently omitted, and in the reign of Richard II their function is reduced to simple consent.

History has thrown no light, as yet, on the way in which the powers of the representatives, whether procuratorial or senatorial, were exercised; and when, in the long political discussions of the fourteenth century, some vestiges of personal independent action can be traced amongst the commons, it is difficult to see that the constitutional position of the representatives in their house differed at all from that of the peers in theirs. It is of course possible that some change for the better followed the definite arrangement of parliament in two houses. In fact, until that arrangement was perfected, the discussion would be monopolised by those members who, by skill in business, greatness of personal position, or fluency in French or Latin, were accustomed to make themselves heard; and few of these would be found amongst the knights, citizens, and burghers. The obscurity of details does not stop here. No authentic record has yet been found of the way in which the general assent of the assembly was taken, or the result of a division ascertained. We might infer from the procuratorial character of the powers of the representatives, that on some questions, taxation in particular, the two members for each community would have only a joint vote. The so-called "Modus tenendi parliamentum" [The Method of Holding Parliament] might be thought likely to illustrate this. But that curious sketch of the parliamentary constitution cannot have been drawn up until a period much later than that on which we are now employed, and seems to describe an ideal of the writer rather than any condition of things that ever really existed.

To this point then had the parliamentary constitution grown under the hand of this great king. The assembly definitely constituted in 1295, — at once a representation of the three estates and a concentration of the local institutions, — the clergy, the barons and the communities, associated for financial, legislative, and political action — obtained in 1297 the fullest recognition of its rights as representing the whole nation. It had come into existence by a growth peculiar to itself, although coinciding in time with the corresponding developments in other nations, and was destined to have a different history. Of this representative body the king was at once the hand and the head, and for foreign affairs the complete inpersonation. He called together the assembly when and where he chose; the result of the deliberations was realised as his act; the laws became valid by his expressed consent, and were enforced under his commission and by his writ; his refusal stayed all proceedings whether legislative or executive. It was no part of the policy of Edward to diminish royal power and dignity; probably for every concession which patriotism or statesmanship led him to make, he retained a check by which the substance of power would be kept in the hand of a sovereign wise enough to use it rightly. The parliamentary constitution was by no means the whole of the English system: there still remained, in varying but not exhausted strength, by no means obsolete, the several institutions royal and popular, central and local, administrative and executive, out of which the parliamentary constitution itself sprang, whose powers it concentrated and regulated but did not extinguish, and whose functions it exercised without superseding them. The general reforms in law, army and finance, which were completed by Edward I, bear the same mark of definiteness and completeness which he so clearly impressed on parliament; a mark which those depart-

ments continued to bear for at least two centuries and a half, and which in some respects they bear to the present day. The permanent and definite character thus impressed gave strength to the system, although it perhaps diminished its elasticity and in some points made the occasion for future difficulties.

The high court of parliament had for one of its historical antecedents the ancient court and council of the king, which was as certainly the parent of the house of lords, as the shire system was of the house of commons. The king's court had in its judicial capacity been the germ of the whole higher judicial system of the country, as well as of the parliamentary and financial machinery. But so far from having lost strength by dividing and subdividing its functions, the magical circle that surrounded the king remained as much as ever a nucleus of strength and light. Such strength and light Edward was well able to appreciate; and in it he found his royal as contrasted with his constitutional position; in other words he organised the powers of his prerogative, the residuum of that royal omnipotence, which, since the days of the Conquest had been on all sides limited by the national growth and by the restrictions imposed by routine, law, policy, and patriotic statesmanship. The primitive constitution, local, popular, self-regulating, had received a new element from the organising power of the Normans. The royal central justice had come to remedy the evils of the popular law; the curia regis was a court of equity in relation to the common law of the county court. Now, the curia regis had incorporated itself with the common law system of the country, just as parliament had become a permanent institution. The royal chancery was now regarded as a resource for equitable remedy against the hardships of the courts of Westminster, as the courts of Westminster had been a remedy against the inequalities of the shiremoot. The vital and prolific power remained unimpaired, and side by side with the growth of the power of parliament, grew also the power of the crown exercised in and through the council. . . .

It would be dangerous to decide by conjecture on a point which has been discussed with so much learning and with such discordant views by many generations of lawyers, when the terms used are in themselves ambiguous and at different periods mean very different things. The fact that the word council implies both an organised body of advisers, and the assembly in which that organised body meets; that it means several differently organised bodies, and the several occasions of their meeting; that those several bodies have themselves different organisations in different reigns although retaining a corporate identity; and that they have frequently been discussed by writers who have been unable to agree on a common vocabulary or proper definitions, has loaded the subject with difficulty. We may however generalise thus: (1) there was a permanent council attendant on the king, and advising him in all his sovereign acts, composed of bishops, barons, judges and others, all sworn as counsellors; and this council sitting in terminal courts assisted the king in hearing suits and receiving petitions. (2) In the parliaments of the three estates, from the year 1295 onwards, the judges and other legal members of this permanent body, who did not possess the right of baronage, were summoned to advise the king. (3) In conjunction with the rest of the prelates and baronage, and excluding the commons and the minor clergy, the permanent council acted sometimes under the title of *magnum concilium;* and this name was, occasionally, given to assemblies in which the council and the Estates met, which are only distinguishable in small technical points from proper parliaments. Many of the assemblies of the reign of Henry III, the constitutions of which we have regarded as steps toward the realisation of the idea of parliament, may be regarded, in the light reflected from the fourteenth century, as examples of the *magnum con-cilium;* but in point of fact the *magnum concilium* under Edward II and Edward III was only a form of the general national assembly which had survived for certain purposes, when for other practical uses of administration it had been superseded by the parliament of the three estates as framed by Edward I. The privy council, from the reign of Richard II onwards, although it inherited and amplified the functions of the permanent council of Edward I, differed widely in its organisation, and the steps by which the difference grew must be discussed later on.

The name of parliament, the king's parliament, belonged to the sessions of each of the three bodies thus distinguished, the terminal session of the select council, the session of the great council, and the session of the commune concilium of the three estates. The historians distinguish between general and special parliaments, the former being the full assembly of the *commune concilium* in the completeness recognised at the moment; the latter the royal session for the dispatch of business. In the Rolls of Parliament the confusion of name and distinction of functions are still more conspicuous, for most of the early documents preserved under that name belong to the sessions of the council for judicial business, held, as the Provisions of Oxford had ordered, at fixed times of the year, and resembling in idea, if not in fact, the crown-wearing days of the Norman kings.

Whilst the constitutional reforms of Edward I were gradually taking their final shape, it is not surprising that some confusion should arise between the functions of the king's council and those of the national council. In both we find the king legislating, judging, deliberating, and taxing, or attempting to tax. If in the one he enacted laws and in the other issued ordinances, if in the one he asked for an aid and in the other imposed a tallage or negotiated the concession of a custom, the ordinance and the statute differed little in application, the voluntary contribution and the arbitrary tallage were demanded with equal cogency from the taxpayer. Some few facts, if not rules or principles may, notwithstanding the rapid changes of the times, be determined, but in general it may be affirmed that for all business, whether it were such as could be done by the king alone or such as required the co-operation of the nation, the action of the smaller circle of advisers was continually employed. The most important points, however, are those connected with judicature and legislation.

The petitions, addressed to the king, or to the king and his council, which are preserved in the early rolls of parliament, furnished abundant work to the permanent council, and the special parliaments were probably the solemn occasions on which they were presented and discussed. These stated sessions were held by Edward I at Hilarytide, Easter, and Michaelmas, or at other times by adjournment. And then were heard also the great placita, or suits which, arising between great men or in unprecedented cases, required the judgment of the king himself; and the general parliaments, which were of course much less frequent, were for the sake of convenience or economy usually called at times when the council was in session; a fact which has increased the difficulty of distinguishing the acts of the two bodies. The placita on these occasions were either relegated to small bodies of auditors who reported their opinion to the council, or were heard in the full council itself. Of the former sort were the suits between the abbot of S. Augustine and the barons of Sandwich in 1280 and between the men of Yarmouth and the Cinque Ports in 1290, in which a small number of councillors were assigned as auditors; of the latter was the claim of Gilbert of Clare to the castle and town of Bristol, and the king's demand of a sentence against Llewelyn, at Michaelmas, 1276, both of which were heard and decided in full council, composed of magnates, justices, and others, whose names are recorded. The hearing of petitions was much more laborious work, and required more minute regulation. In the eighth year of Edward I it was ordered that all petitions should be examined by the judges of the court to which the matter in question properly belonged, so that only important questions should be brought before the king and council, especially such as were matters of grace and favour which could not be answered without reference to the king. A further order of the twenty-first year provided that these petitions should be divided, by the persons assigned to receive them, into five bundles, containing severally the documents to be referred to the Chancery, the Exchequer, the judges, the king and council, and those which had been already answered, so that matters referred to the king himself might be laid before him before he proceeded to transact business. For the hearing as well as the reception of these petitions provision was made in the parliament, or by the king before the parliament opened; and from the records of 1305 we find that they were now presented in the full parliament of the estates, for in that year Edward named special commissions of judges and barons to receive the petitions touching Scotland, Gascony, Ireland, and the Channel Islands. Those which could not be answered without reference to the king formed a special branch of business, and it was from the share taken by the Chancellor in examining and reporting on the bills of grace and favour that his equitable jurisdiction in the fourteenth century grew up. The nomination of receivers and triers became a part of the opening business of every parliament, and the ultimate division of the work, in the reign of Richard II, was into three portions, one for the king, one for the council, and one for the parliament itself.

Edward I, in the preamble of several of his statutes, some of which were distinctly the result of deliberation of the general parliament, mentions the participation of the council as well as that of the assembled estates. The first statute of Westminster was enacted by the king *par son conseil* [by his council], and by the assent of the magnates and community: the statute *de religiosis* [Statute of Mortmain, 1279] is made *de consilio praelatorum comitum et aliorum fidelium regni nostri de consilio nostro existentium* [by the advice of our prelates, earls, barons, and other faithful men of our realm who are our council]; the statute, so called, of Acton Burnell is an enactment by the king, *par luy e par sun conseil a sun parlement* [by himself and his council at his parliament]. In such cases it seems impossible to understand by the *conseil* merely the advice of the persons who are afterwards said to have consented. In other cases, however, the king enacts, or ordains by his council when the action of parliament is altogether unnoticed. The statute of Rageman is "accorded by the king and by his council"; the statute "de Bigamis" rehearses the names of a sort of committee of councillors, in whose presence the draught of it was read before it was confirmed by the king and the entire council. It would seem certain from this that the king in his council made ordinances, as by the advice of his council he enacted laws with consent of parliament. All Edward's legislation may be received as of full and equal authority, but we have to look forward to days in which the distinction between statute and ordinance will be closely scrutinised.

# Parliament as an Occasion for the Dispensing of Justice

## FREDERICK WILLIAM MAITLAND

While Stubbs was praising parliament, Frederick William Maitland (1850–1906) was showing England the splendid history of its legal institutions. With Frederick Pollock, he published in 1895 *The History of English Law before the Time of Edward I*, and in 1908 Maitland's classroom lectures at Cambridge were posthumously printed as *The Constitutional History of England*. Like Stubbs, he stressed the importance of writing history from the sources; he began the Selden Society publications because the medieval Year Books were inaccurate. Maitland's skill in recreating the thoughts and actions of medieval men is unsurpassed; R. L. Schuyler called him "the historical spirit incarnate." In the selection below, taken from his introduction to the *Memoranda de Parliamento* (the parliament roll of 1305), Maitland suggests that in early parliaments, officials of the king's council played a more vital role than the representatives of the three estates.

ON THE 12TH OF NOVEMBER 1304 King Edward issued from Burstwick writs for a parliament to be holden at Westminster on the 16th of February 1305. He was on his way back from Scotland. He kept Christmas at Lincoln and was there as late as the 12th of January. On the 22nd he was at Spalding and thence issued a second set of writs. Events, he said, had happened which made it impossible for him to be at Westminster on the appointed day, so the parliament was post-

From F. W. Maitland, ed., *Memoranda de Parliamento* (Rolls Series, 1893), xxxiv–xxxviii, xlvii–1, liii, lv–lvi, lxvi–lxviii, lxxv–lxxvii, lxxix, lxxxiv–lxxxv, lxxxviii.

poned to the 28th of February. Slowly and by a circuitous route he travelled southward, for we hear of him at Walsingham, Swaffham, Thetford, Bury St. Edmunds, Exning, Wilbraham, Royston, Braughing, Standon, Wades Hill, Ware, Waltham. On the 26th of January he addressed a letter under his privy seal to the chancellor, which may perhaps explain the postponement. He expected that in the ensuing parliament the clergy would call him in question and he directed that a search should be made in the chancery for any documents which might bear upon the matters in dispute. By other letters under the privy seal dated on the 5th of February . . . he directed the appointment of receivers and auditors of petitions; he desired that the petitions should, so far as was possible, be disposed of before his arrival at Westminster. Meanwhile the sheriffs of Kent, Surrey and Sussex had been bidden to send up great quantities of corn and ale to Westminster for the maintenance of the king's household. On the 27th he entered London and stayed at the Hospital of St. Katharine near the Tower. On the 28th the parliament was opened at Westminster.

It was a full parliament in our sense of that term. The three estates of the realm met the king and his council. The great precedent of 1295 had been followed and, if the writs of summons were punctually obeyed, the assembly was a large one. By rights there should have been present some ninety-five prelates, about a hundred and forty-five representatives of the inferior clergy, nine earls (if we include the Prince of Wales and the Earl of Angus), ninety-four barons, seventy-four knights of the shires, and about two hundred citizens and burgesses; altogether some six hundred men. Besides these we must take account of thirty-three members of the king's council to whom writs were sent, and . . . there were yet other men present and performing important duties, men who had a special knowledge of Scotland and Gascony.

This assembly was kept together for just three weeks. On the 21st of March a proclamation was made telling the archbishops, bishops and other prelates, earls, barons, knights, citizens and burgesses in general that they might go home, but must be ready to appear again if the king summoned them. Those bishops, earls, barons, justices and others who were members of the council were to remain behind and so were all those who had still any business to transact. But the "parliament" was not at an end. Many of its doings that are recorded on our roll were done after the estates had been sent home. The king remained at Westminster, surrounded by his councillors, and his parliament was still in session as a "full" and "general" parliament as late as the 5th and 6th of April. . . .

Now if we are to frame any exact conception of the body or various bodies of men by whom the business that is recorded on our roll was transacted, and of the mode in which they dealt with that business, it seems necessary that we should understand the composition of the king's council. Unfortunately, as is well known, the council of Edward I is still for us an ill-defined group of men. Writs of summons and writs for wages will often teach us the names of all the barons who were called to a parliament and enable us to know who it was that represented the pettiest boroughs, and yet we cannot enumerate with any certainty the members of the council. We can indeed make a list of those of its members who, not being prelates or barons, were summoned by name to be present at a given parliament. On the present occasion no less than thirty-three men were thus summoned. The list included Phillip Willoughby the chancellor of the exchequer, the justices of the two benches and the barons of the exchequer, several men who were being employed as justices in eyre and thirteen masters of the chancery or clerks of the councils. . . . The chancery is still the great secretarial department; it does nearly all the king's writing for him, whether such writing concerns foreign affairs or the government of England. If for a moment we may use such modern terms, we may say that the chancery is Home Office, Foreign Office, Board of Trade, Local Government Board all in one; in short it is a general secretarial bureau, which exercises a certain control even over the only other great official "department" that there is, namely the exchequer. Thus when the king is surrounded by the masters or principal clerks of the chancery, he has at his side the men who know most about the way in which England is governed and foreign affairs are managed, "permanent" or fairly permanent, "under-secretaries of state," and yet men who are on their promotion, for some of them may well look to being chancellors or treasurers before they die. It is among them also that the king finds his diplomatists. The thirty-three names therefore upon our list represent almost all that England has to show in the way of legal learning, official experience, and administrative ability.

But then of course it is certain that there are members of the council who are not upon this list. They have been otherwise summoned. . . . When, however, all due allowance has been made for all our doubts and mistakes, we have to picture to ourselves the council as being in the main a body of officers, of ministers, of men who in one capacity or another are doing the king's work and receiving the king's pay. . . . A full meeting of the council is a full meeting of the king's bench, of the common bench, of the chancery, of the exchequer: it is this and more than this. . . .

And now we may ask the question, what does our record tell us of the part played in this parliament by the king's council, and by those who constituted or represented the three estates of the realm? We may bring the business of a medieval parliament under five heads, namely — (1) the discussion of affairs of state, more especially foreign affairs; (2) legislation; (3) taxation or supply; (4) the audience of petitions; (5) judicial business, the determination of causes criminal and civil.

The king had summoned the estates in order that he might treat "of certain matters specially touching our realm of England and the establishment of our land of Scotland," and no doubt the state of Scotland was one of the main matters which required his attention and the advice of his councillors. . . . Whether Edward had sought advice in this matter from the mass of the clergy, baronage, and commoners, we cannot say; nor do we know that the affairs of Gascony afforded material for a general debate. . . .

In the way of legislation this parliament did little. No statute was passed which at once found a place upon the statute roll. . . . As to taxation, we have every reason to believe that on the present occasion no tax of any kind was imposed, and we have no evidence to show that the king asked for money. . . .

But by far the greater part of our parliament roll is occupied by entries which concern the audience of petitions. Before we discuss any of the many questions which such entries suggest we must remember that many of the original petitions exist, and the external form of a petition should be briefly described.

It will in general be a strip of parchment about five inches long, while its breadth will vary from three inches to a bare inch. On the front of this strip and along its length the petitioner's grievance and prayer will be written, usually in French, rarely in Latin, and will be addressed "to our lord the king" or "to our lord the king and his council." On the back of this strip and across its breadth there will almost always be written some words, usually in Latin, rarely at this time in French, which either prescribe the relief which the petitioner is to have or send him away empty. . . .

We know that for some time past the multitude of petitions presented at the king's parliaments had been giving trouble and had been met by various expedients. In the eighth year of the reign we hear that "the folk who come to the king's parliament are often delayed and disturbed to the great grievance of them and of the court by the numerous petitions which are presented to the king, many of which might be 'exploited' before the chancellor and the justices." It is, therefore, provided that these petitions are to be sorted. Those which concern the seal are to come before the chancellor, others are to be sent according to their nature to the exchequer or to the justices, or to the justices of the Jewry. Only those "which are so great or so much of grace" that they cannot otherwise be dealt with, are to come before the king in order that his pleasure may be taken, and they are to be brought before him and his council by the chancellor and the other chief ministers, so that he and his council may have leisure to attend to the great affairs of his realm and of other lands. Then in the twenty-first year it was ordained that all petitions which thenceforth should be proffered at the parliaments should be handed in to receivers appointed by the king in order that they might be examined. Five bundles were to be made, one for the chancery, another for the exchequer, a third for the justices, a fourth for the king and his council, while the fifth was to contain those which had already been answered. . . .

The petitions of which our roll speaks are neither petitions by parliament nor yet are they petitions addressed to parliament. We see at once that they are very different from those petitions of the commons (*petitions de la commune, petitions des communes*) which will occupy the greater part of almost any parliament roll of Edward III's day. But again they are not addressed to "parliament," or to "the lords of parliament," or to either house of parliament. They are addressed either "to the king" or "to the king and his council." In a certain sense they are parliamentary petitions, they are presented in or at a parliament. But at present "parliament" or "a parliament" is not conceived as a body that can be petitioned. A parliament is rather an act than a body of persons. One cannot present a petition to a colloquy, to a debate. It is but slowly that this word is appropriated to

colloquies of a particular kind, namely, those which the king has with the estates of his realm, and still more slowly that it is transferred from the colloquy to the body of men whom the king has summoned. As yet any meeting of the king's council that has been solemnly summoned for general business seems to be a parliament. These petitions are not addressed to parliament, nor are they addressed to the assembled estates, nor are they addressed to the earls, barons, and prelates. They are addressed either simply to the king or to the king and his council. The formal title for them which is in use in the chancery is "petitiones de consilio," "council petitions."

When we examine the character of these petitions we soon see that for the more part they were not fit subjects for discussion in a large assembly. They do not ask for anything that could be called legislation; the responses that are given to them are in no sort "private acts of parliament." Generally the boon that is asked for is one which the king without transcending his legal powers might either grant or deny. Sometimes we may say that, if the facts are truly stated by the petitioner, the king is more or less strictly bound by the rules of common honesty to give him some relief: — The king owes him wages, or his lands have been wrongfully seized by the king's officers. At other times what is asked for is pure grace and favour: — The petitioner owes the king money and asks that he may be allowed to pay it by instalments, or that in consideration of his poverty part of his debt may be forgiven, or perhaps the University of Cambridge asks that the king will found a college. . . .

As to what was done by the assembled commoners during the three weeks that they spent at Westminster, we shall hardly get beyond guesswork. All that we learn from our roll is, first, that they joined in a petition with the magnates about the exportation of the wealth of the monasteries, to which petition the king gave his assent, though he did not at once convert it into a statute; and secondly, that they presented two petitions of their own, which were refused. The king, so far as we know, did not ask them for money, nor did he desire their consent to any new law. The doctrine that in these days the representatives of the shires and towns were called to parliament not in order that they might act in concert on behalf of the commons of England, but in order that each might represent before the king in council the grievances and the interests of the particular community, county or borough, that sent him thither, may easily be pressed too far, but we shall probably think that there is no little truth in it, if we ask what the knights and burgesses were doing while the king and his councillors were slowly disposing of this great mass of petitions, many of which were presented by shires and boroughs. Official testimony the council can easily obtain; but it wants unofficial testimony also; it desires to know what men are saying in remote parts of England about the doings of sheriffs, escheators, and their like, and the possibilities of future taxation have to be considered. Then, again, there are many appointments to be made; for example, it is the fashion at this time to entrust a share in the work of delivering the county gaol to some knight of the county, very often to one of the knights who is representing or has represented that county at a parliament. Without denying that the germ of a "house" of commons already exists, without denying that its members hold meetings, discuss their common affairs and common grievances, without denying that Edward has encouraged them to do this — at the present moment he has a quarrel with the clergy, at least with the archbishop, and no doubt is glad when the assembled commons protest that there are abuses in the church — without denying all this, we may still believe that the council often gives audience, advice, instructions to particular knights and burgesses. After all we have to fall back upon the words of the writ of summons: — the commoners have been told to come in order that they may do what shall be ordained. . . .

We pass to judicial business, noticing that the line between this and the hearing of petitions is not very sharp. The *Placita* which came before this parliament were few but miscellaneous.

In the first place we have the very famous [treason] case of Nicholas Segrave. . . . He confessed this grave offence. . . . The king, however . . . was content that Segrave should find seven manucaptors who would undertake that he would render himself to prison if ever the king should call upon him to do so. . . . Segrave's manucaptors appeared "before the king and his council" on the 29th of March. . . . The assembly of the estates had been dissolved on the 21st. . . .

A citizen of Bayonne, a hostage in the king's hand, had been committed to the care of the citizens of Winchester, but had escaped. For his escape the citizens were to answer by their . . . representatives "before us and our council in our forthcoming parliament at Westminster." . . .

Such records as these — and many others of a like kind might be cited from other rolls — bring us within sight of an often debated and still debateable question. What in Edward I's day was the jurisdictional competence of the king's council? . . . We are dealing with something that is new. . . . Fleta uses vague words about it. . . . Seemingly all that we dare say is that the causes heard in parliament are important causes, important because they concern the king, or because they concern very great men, or because they involve grave questions of public law, or because they are unprecedented. We must not miss the "equitableness" of this tribunal. When Fleta says that it provides new remedies for new wrongs, and that justice is done to every man according to his deserts, he means that this supreme court can look at "the merits of the case" with some disregard for technicalities. We are dealing with a court that has large, indefinite powers. . . .

Perhaps more than enough has already been said about these controverted matters; but it seemed necessary to remind readers, who are conversant with the "parliaments" of later days, that about the parliaments of Edward I's time there is still much to be discovered, and that should they come to the opinion that a session of the king's council is the core and essence of every *parliamentum,* that the documents usually called "parliamentary petitions" are petitions to the king and his council, that the auditors of petitions are committees of the council, that the rolls of parliament are the records of the business done by the council, — sometimes with, but much more often without, the concurrence of the estates of the realm, — that the highest tribunal in England is not a general assembly of barons and prelates, but the king's council, they will not be departing very far from the path marked out by books that are already classical.

# Law-Declaring in Parliament

## CHARLES HOWARD MCILWAIN

Charles Howard McIlwain (1871–     ) approached parliament through the history of legal and political thought, which he taught at Harvard. Among his published works are *The Growth of Political Thought in the West* (1932), and *The American Revolution: A Constitutional Interpretation,* winner of the Pulitzer Prize for American history in 1924. McIlwain also wrote "Medieval Estates" for the *Cambridge Medieval History* (1932), an entry that admirably combines the English and Continental origins of representative assemblies. In the selection below, taken from his *High Court of Parliament and Its Supremacy,* McIlwain argues that the English parliament was in its origins a high court, whose "legislative" functions consisted only in defining the meaning of customary law.

THE ROLLS OF PARLIAMENT show that a large part of the work of the "Parliament" was what we should call "judicial," consisting of those cases that had proved too hard or too novel for the judges in the separate courts. Obviously this would be no kind of business for the untrained "aliis incolis regni" [other inhabitants of the realm]. So the cases were settled before these came to give their advice or their money, or were left until they had gone home again. As the bulk of early "legislation" — if we may use such a term — was only "novis injuriis emersis nova . . . remedia" [new remedies [provided] when new injuries arise], limited in amount and exceptional in character, most of the business of a session must have been of such a nature that it could be done only by "The King's Council in his Parliament." Thus the "Commons," when we find a Commons, may have lent their authority to Parliament, but in practice at first had but little influence over much of its activity. This explanation, though in part conjectural, may serve in some degree to remove the apparent inconsistency resulting from the indiscriminate use by contemporary writers of such terms as *Consilium* and *Curia Regis* for so many different things.

Undoubtedly one reason why we cannot

From Charles H. McIlwain, *The High Court of Parliament and Its Supremacy* (New Haven, 1910, Bailey Bros. and Swinfen edition, London, 1963), pp. 25–27, 109–121. Reprinted by permission of Yale University Press.

get a clearer-cut picture of the great central courts at this time is the indefiniteness that we find in the names employed to designate these courts and their activities in contemporary accounts and records, — an indefiniteness in words which is only proof of the indefiniteness of the thought of the men of that day, and an indication of a corresponding absence of special organization in the institutions they described. It is next to impossible to define such institutions exactly without making the definition untrue to the facts. In a picture of the institutions of mediaeval times we must be satisfied with hazy outlines. If in such a picture we demand all· the sharpness of figure and detail that we might reasonably expect when modern institutions are described, we deceive ourselves; for such details can be supplied at this late day only by giving words a definite sense, but it may be one that they never had in the minds of the men that used them. The result may be artistic: it will not be truthful.

\*     \*     \*

The word *Parliament* has come to carry with it the idea of a lawmaking assembly of the type described by Blackstone. Men in time became so familiar with that idea that they were not conscious of the great and unwarranted assumption they were making when speaking of Tudor and pre-Tudor times; for Parliament, up to the time of the Tudors, was hardly thought of primarily or principally as a legislature: it was still in reality "The High Court of Parliament." That court then retained the varied functions of the old Curia, as Parliament now does; but the judicial functions bulked larger in men's minds than the legislative. Parliament still seemed primarily a law-declaring machine. So long as the law was a thing fundamental and immutable, "a subject of science, capable of being learnt by special study, but not capable of being altered by the mere will of government," Parliament's functions must have been conceived to be in large part merely the enforcing and applying of

this law: Parliament must have been thought of first as a court rather than as a legislature. This I believe to have been the view prevailing, among lawyers at least, as late as the assembling of the Long Parliament. The statement of James I and Bacon, that a judge's functions were rather *jus dicere* than *jus dare* [to speak or say the law, rather than to give the law], would have seemed as properly applicable to the High Court of Parliament, if not so fully, as to the courts at Westminster Hall. The prominence of the judicial character of Parliament in the minds of men of the mediaeval period is the normal and natural consequence of the prevailing view that law was fixed; but it is at times surprising to find how late that idea has survived, how many of the characteristics even of the modern sovereign Parliament are due to it, and how many of the great parliamentary struggles of comparatively recent times have been influenced by the old conception of Parliament as a court.

"The function of a court of law," says Gneist, "was and remained the very kernel of every Germanic form of Constitution; judicial proceedings formed the current business of every national assembly." Such a "national assembly" as England could be said to have had in the period of the Norman kings was "rather a court than an organized council." The fact, already noted, of the frequent use of the word *curia* [court] for such assemblies is strong proof of this. Hoveden [medieval chronicler] uses that word for the assembly in which the Constitutions of Clarendon were drawn up in 1164.

Another proof, and a striking one, of the judicial character of the Council is afforded by the dispute between the kings of Castile and Navarre, which they agreed should be settled by a *"judicium"* [judgment], *"in curia . . . regis Angliae"* [in the court of the English king], in 1177.

The Statute of Merton in 1235 is said in the preamble to be made *"in Curia Domini Regis"* [in the Court of the Lord King]. Under Edward I the same conditions remain: Parliament is still "pre-eminently intended to be a judicial assembly, to which the other functions are annexed." An instance in this reign similar in some respects to that of the kings of Navarre and Castile under Henry II was the famous award in the case of the disputed Scotch succession in 1292.

In 1322 the famous "Colloquium" met at York which revoked the ordinances made by the barons in 1310, and declared that in future such matters "shall be treated accorded and established in Parliaments by our Lord the King, and by the assent of the Prelates, Earls and Barons, and the Commonalty of the Realm." This has often been considered "the first express recognition of Parliament as a legislative assembly."

Whether this be true or not, generations had yet to pass before the old "judicial" functions of Parliament gave way to the legislative. In fact, in the ordinances made in 1311 it is expressly stated that Parliament must be held once a year, or twice if necessary, for hearing pleas, including those "whereon the Justices are of divers Opinions."

The oaths that were taken by the members of the Council show how much emphasis was placed upon matters judicial. This judicial character of Parliament also appears in many other ways. It appears in the practice of holding the Parliament on legal term days, which went back to the Saxon times. To it may be attributed, in some degree at least, the exemption of peers from jury service. There was, in fact, in feudal times no sharp line drawn between public and private rights. Indeed, from one point of view, the very essence of feudalism was this fusion of public and private rights. And as with rights, so with their infringement and the manner of remedy. Wrongs against individuals were not clearly divided from crimes. This is probably the most characteristic feature common to the different *Leges Barbarorum*, and it survived to be a central fact of feudalism. Punishment of a private wrong in

like manner is often indistinguishable from the punishment of an offence which we consider to be mainly against the state. Thus, as will be shown in greater detail later, there is no definite line that can be drawn between statute and ordinance, on the one hand, or even between an act and an "award" of Parliament. The determining of a suit between parties and the granting of a petition, whether the petition came from an individual, or a class, or the Commons, are alike "acts" of Parliament, and of equal force and dignity. A study of the controversial writings of the seventeenth century shows that even then, when an act of Parliament was passed overriding a judicial decision of the Lords, the whole Parliament was considered to be above the Lords, — an idea that does not occur to us to-day because we distinguish the judicial supremacy of the Lords from the legislative supremacy of Parliament. In the middle ages the boundary is indistinguishable between "acts" of Parliament that are particular and acts that are general, between acts that are private and acts that are public, between acts administrative, acts legislative, and acts judicial. Only gradually do these distinctions appear; and for a long period after they do, it is the judicial functions of the Assembly that dwarf the others. The Statute of Bigamy of 4 Edward I was in the character of a judicial interpretation of the words of a general council of the Church.

A celebrated clause in the Statute of Westminster Second is significant: "And whensoever from henceforth it shall fortune in the Chancery, that in one Case a Writ is found, and in like Case falling under like Law, and requiring like Remedy, is found none, the Clerks of the Chancery shall agree in making the Writ; or the Plaintiffs may adjourn it until the next Parliament, and let the Cases be written in which they cannot agree, and let them refer themselves until the next Parliament, and let a writ be made by the advice of the learned in the law lest it should happen in future that the court should long time fail to minister Justice unto complainants." Evidently, in this case, as Mr. Holdsworth says, "it is not clear whether the clause refers to the judicial or to the legislative powers of Parliament, because at that time the line was not clearly drawn between these distinct powers." A regular means of carrying this enactment into effect seems the object of the provision made at the Parliament of Lincoln in 1315, where the Chancellor, the Treasurer, and the judges of both benches are commanded to draw up a record of all cases pending before them "which cannot be determined outside of Parliament," and to refer the same to Parliament for adjudication. Edward III's Statute of Treasons contains the following striking provision: "And because that many other like Cases of Treason may happen in Time to come, which a Man cannot think nor declare at this present Time; it is accorded, That if any other Case, Supposed treason, which is not above specified, doth happen before any Justices, the Justices shall tarry without any going to Judgement of the Treason, till the Cause be shewed and declared before the King and his Parliament whether it ought to be judged Treason or other Felony."

In 1 Richard II, the Commons petitioned the King to hold a Parliament at least once a year for the hearing of cases where injustice had been done on account of delays in the King's Courts or where the judges could not agree.

This fusion of functions, as may be expected, can be traced through abundant instances in legal records from Bracton's time on. Such a view of Parliament, however, was not confined to lawyers in the later mediaeval period, as is indicated by the passage in the *Vision of Piers the Plowman*, where Peace is represented as coming into Parliament to "putte up a bylle" against Wrong, charging seduction and rape. Parliament was called together in those times, as Palgrave[2] says,

[2] Francis Palgrave edited *Parliamentary Writs and Writs of Military Summons* for the Record Commission, 1827–1834. [Editor's note.]

not only for the purposes of legislation or taxation, but to the intent that the complaints either of the commonwealth, or of individuals, might be discussed and heard. It was the King's great and extraordinary court of justice, in which he was to grant redress when the ordinary tribunals were unable or unwilling to grant relief. Frequent Parliaments were required, because justice could not be administered without these assemblies. It was only in Parliament that the doubts of the learned in the law could be solved, and the obstacles impeding the due course of the law be removed.

When the common-law became inefficient, the supreme remedial jurisdiction was vested in the High Court of Parliament. Here the people were invited to resort for the redress of all injuries and oppressions not cognizable elsewhere; and the inability of the petitioner to sue at common law, or to obtain a fair trial by jury, according to the ordinary process, is the most common allegation in the petitions.

When we thus speak of Parliament as a "court of justice" and designate its actions as "judicial," it will be remembered that "court" and "judicial' are not to be used in their modern definite sense. We can never understand the institutions of mediaeval England if we consider Parliament as a "court of justice" which *in addition* exercised other distinct powers, or as a legislature with an addendum of other duties. It is the *fusion* of indefinite powers which is the most fundamental fact in English central institutions in the middle ages. It will be seen that this applies not to Parliament merely, but to all the other courts of the King as well, and it thus furnishes the key to the great problem which claims our main attention in this essay, — the relations existing between the King's High Court of Parliament and his other courts.

It must have been noticed that the instances cited above, many of them, refer to a period after the law courts and the Privy Council were definitely established as separate judicial tribunals. These bodies when they came into existence only shared with the Parliament in the "judicial" business; they did not supersede it. In fact, as we have seen, the line between the "jurisdiction" of Parliament and that of the other courts cannot be laid down, and that because it was not clearly perceived nor any necessity for it appreciated. Using "court" in the sense above noted, we may say, then, that the High Court of Parliament, though the greatest of the courts, was still a court; and if its higher dignity and representative character gave it the power to lay down a new rule when no old one could be found that was applicable, this power, though great and unique, was really only incidental, and neither new nor startling. It required time, a long time, and great changes in the state — the decline of class feeling, a wider distribution of wealth and culture and a widening political self-consciousness in consequence, a change in the conception of kingship, along with sharp controversies ecclesiastical and civil — to alter all this and subordinate the old idea of a court to the newer one of a legislature. It is the persistence of this old idea, notwithstanding the great changes, which is the important thing. Parliament has retained somewhat the character of a court while it has taken on the new duties of a legislature. Hardly anyone will deny the eminently judicial cast of Parliament in the middle ages; few have considered the importance of Parliament's retention of those judicial characteristics, after the other law courts grew into a separate existence, and fewer have reckoned with their influence upon the modern development and present form of parliamentary institutions, English and American. It is therefore this more modern phase of the history of the High Court which especially needs proof and illustration. It is believed that sufficient proofs do exist, and it is hoped that they can be here shown, to warrant the conviction expressed by Palgrave that "the character of the English parliament as a supreme court of remedial jurisdiction has never altered though many changes have taken place in its form."

# Justice as the Essence of Parliamentary Business

## HENRY GERALD RICHARDSON
## GEORGE OSBORNE SAYLES

The combined research of H. G. Richardson (1884– ) and G. O. Sayles (1901– ) has produced elaborate evidence in support of the judicial-administrative theory of parliamentary origins. Since 1928 these two scholars have edited parliamentary rolls for the Camden Society and plea rolls for the Selden Society; a succession of joint articles has appeared in such journals as the *Bulletin of the Institute of Historical Research*, the *Royal Historical Society Transactions*, the *Law Quarterly Review*, and the *English Historical Review*. Sayles published *The Medieval Foundations of England* in 1950, and together the two men have recently (1964) completed *The Governance of Medieval England*. The latter book contains a provocative interpretation of "William Stubbs: the Man and the Historian." The selection below, written for the *Law Quarterly Review* in 1961, is both a restatement of their views on parliamentary origins and an answer to their critics.

I F THERE WAS an undeniable likeness between parliaments and great councils, why then do we lay stress upon the difference between them? It is because, as we have said, the difference is fundamental. We believe, let us repeat, "that parliaments are of one kind only and that . . . the essence of them is the dispensing of justice." If this were not so, it would be difficult to understand why the author of *Fleta* should have described parliament as he did or how the Ordainers could have obtained the conception of parliament that patently informed their decisions on the functions to be discharged in future parliaments. It would be equally difficult to understand why the surviving records of the parliaments of the first two Edwards (the period with which we were primarily concerned when we first used the words we cite) are so overwhelmingly the result of the dispensation of justice. If we were writing of a later period, we would not employ quite the same words, though they apply with equal force to the early years of Edward III. . . .

Now, despite the wealth of contemporary authority, our conclusions on the nature and function of parliament have been challenged. To disarm criticism we might perhaps have claimed, in the ironical phrase of Maitland's, that we were "not departing very far from the path marked out by books that are already classical." Did not the Lords Committees[1] declare, in the light of the evidence known to them, that in the reigns of Henry III and Edward I parliament was the name given to "an assembly . . . acting generally as the king's ordinary council or as a court of justice"? Did not Stubbs take the same view when he stated the obvious truth that "most of the early documents preserved under that name [sc. the Rolls of Parliament] belong to the sessions of the council for judicial business"? We do no more than assert that there were not several kinds of

[1] *Reports from the Lords Committees Appointed to Search the Journals of the House, Rolls of Parliament and Other Records and Documents, for all Matters Touching the Dignity of a Peer of the Realm*, 4 volumes (Record Commission, 1820–1825). [Editor's note.]

From H. G. Richardson and G. O. Sayles, "Parliaments and Great Councils in Medieval England," *Law Quarterly Review*, LXXVII (1961), pp. 407–417, 419–423, 426. Reprinted by permission of Stevens & Sons Ltd., Publishers.

parliament, as classical teaching held, but one kind only and that if some parliaments were "general" — the contemporary adjective for those more numerously attended — they were nevertheless "ordinary" parliaments. Why then should the difference between the classical position and our own appear so wide? Is it not because we reject in its totality Stubbs's conception of a "parliamentary constitution" as "the English system" of government in the Middle Ages, even though the qualification be added that this "was by no means the whole of the system."

In the dust of controversy there seems to be some likelihood that Stubbs's own teaching may be obscured. Let us then recall his words. "We must be content," he said, "to understand by the name of parliament all meetings of the national council called together in the form that was usual at that particular time." By implication he plainly excluded "the sessions of the council for judicial business" which were nevertheless called by contemporaries parliaments and which were "held, as the Provisions of Oxford had ordered, at fixed times of the year." Under "the parliamentary constitution . . . the clergy, the barons and the communities" were "associated for financial, legislative and political action," and, whatever had been the shortcomings in the past, the parliament of 1295 "was to be a model assembly . . . serving as a pattern for all future assemblies of the nation" or, as Stubbs said elsewhere, was "a perfect representation of the three estates . . . and a parliament constituted on the model of which every succeeding assembly bearing that name was formed." The diffuseness of Stubbs's exposition and his neglect to resolve apparent inconsistencies between statements made in different contexts render it far from easy to form a coherent picture of the parliament of his imagination. We have done our best, by piecing together passages sometimes wide apart, to present a true and intelligible account, without, we trust, distortion or misrepresen-

tation. This, at least, can be said: not the most ingenious of interpretations can reconcile Stubbs's conception of parliament with *Fleta's* — the conception of parliament where "the king in council holds his court in the presence of prelates, earls, barons, nobles and others learned in the law." Stubbs's parliament is not conciliar in this sense: his parliament is a national council, "the concentration of the three estates." Nor, in Stubbs's view, were the representatives of the commons on an inferior footing to the other "estates": "under Edward II, Edward III and Richard II," he asserted, "the third estate claimed and won its place as the foremost of the three." The picture thus presented is not one of the English parliament of contemporary documents, not the parliament of history, but something imaginary masquerading as history. It is, if you will, anachronistic, a projecting into the past of a "parliamentary constitution" which Stubbs believed, without justification, to have existed in the later Middle Ages.

One of the curiosities of historiography is that, just as French scholars have been inclined to minimise the part played by the thirteenth-century parliament of Paris in administrative and political matters, so English scholars have tried to wish away the judicial functions of the early English parliament. Stubbs was nearer to the truth than he imagined when he said that "the parliament of Paris [under Philippe le Bel] may be generally compared with the special judicial session or parliament of the council" or, again, "the point at which the two constitutions approximated more nearly than at any other in the middle ages" was the end of Edward I's reign in England and the reign of Philippe le Bel in France. It may seem astonishing that Stubbs could approach so near to the realities of history and yet persist in his dogma of an English "parliamentary constitution," which falsifies his teaching throughout. He could, indeed, keep himself in countenance only by asserting that parliaments were of three kinds and then, because the records did not bear him, out, abusing the Rolls of Parliament for their confusion.

It may be that, like A. F. Pollard, we are "insufficiently appreciative of the genius of Stubbs" and, truth to tell, we are unimpressed by the attempts that have been made to justify his teaching. But let us examine the case that has lately been made against us. It has been said that the Provisions of Oxford describe the "function" of "pre-representative parliaments" — those, we take it, which were not, in Stubbs's phrase, "national councils" — and are inconsistent with our views. This, however, is to misunderstand the clause . . . [in the Provisions of Oxford] which prescribes that the "elected councillors" are to be present in parliament to survey the state of the realm and to discuss the common interests of the king and the kingdom. We agree that these terms, "le estat du reaume" and "les communes busoignes du roy et du reaume" — which we have elsewhere suggested might be rendered as "high politics" and "public affairs" — are much wider than the dispensing of justice, but the comment is irrelevant. The clause is not intended to describe the function of parliament. . . . We have therefore to turn to other documents to learn something of this aspect of the Oxford parliament [June, 1258] and its successors.

We look first at the Petition of the Barons which preceded the Oxford Parliament. Doubtless some of the clauses called for what we should term administrative action, but for the most part what was demanded was a change either in the administration of the law or in the law itself, a demand for what Bracton, who had just laid down his pen, would have called justice. And then in the parliament itself two noteworthy decisions were taken. One was to invite complaints of injustice from · every aggrieved person in every county: these plaints were to be reduced to writing and presented to the justiciar in his eyre. The other was to instruct the judges and

others learned in the law to consider before the next parliament "what ill laws and need of reformation there were." At a later stage it was decided that the knights in each county, responsible for enrolling plaints, should appear before the council with their inquests in the following Michaelmas parliament; precisely what then happened is not clear, though evidently nothing more could be done by the council in parliament than to expedite the hearing and determining of the plaints. Of the labours of the judges we know more, for they resulted in the Provisions of Westminster, which were promulgated in the Michaelmas parliament of 1259 and, after some vicissitudes, achieved statutory form at Marlborough in 1267. It is true that these two matters were but two items in a wide programme of reform, which covered as well the Church, the Jewry and the royal households, but they were the two items which were pursued from parliament to parliament and they represent what everyone would agree was parliamentary business under Edward I. The other items we have named were not ordinary items of parliamentary business, for the Oxford parliament was a very unusual parliament, one to which, in Henry III's words, men came sworn "ad reformacionem status regni nostri" [for the reforming of the state of our kingdom]. This is not the purpose for which a medieval king normally summoned his parliament. And it is noteworthy that amidst all the discussion of high policy, the tempestuous debates between the king's friends and the dissident barons at Oxford, time was found for the hearing of an action that had been removed from the bench at Dublin. This, indeed, was such an action as was placed in the forefront of parliamentary business by the Ordainers, an action that had been delayed because the defendant pleaded that he could not answer without the king. It is difficult to conceive of any better evidence both of the continuity of parliamentary practice and of the truth that the dispensing of justice is of the essence of parliament.

Of the parliaments held between 1258 and 1272 we have, with rare exceptions, few details. . . .

Doubtless, when unprinted records are further explored, we shall get more light on the parliaments of Henry III, but we know enough to perceive that there is no discontinuity, that justice is dispensed there. Had it not been so, the character of Edward I's parliaments would have been inexplicable. It is remarkable, however, that none of the few petitions which have survived from Henry III's reign can be identified with any of his parliaments, while the flow of parliamentary petitions begins very early, if not from the outset, under Edward I. And at this point we must confront another difficulty that has been raised. Do not these petitions ask for the king's grace and do not many of them ask for something else than a judicial remedy? There is available the analysis of the petitions which Maitland edited: they do not all belong to one parliament, as he supposed, but they may be accepted as a good random sample for the early years of the fourteenth century. Apart from five "petitions of a general character by the estates of the realm" — words we should hesitate to adopt — the petitions fall into three groups: (a) petitions for legal relief in cases in which the king is concerned; (b) petitions for favours to be granted by the king; (c) petitions relating to private wrongs. With few exceptions the petitions in classes (a) and (c) ask for what may fairly be described as judicial remedies. Even in class (b) there are a good many which ask for relief from the consequences of the administration of justice or the operation of the law: pardon of penalties, delivery from gaol, leave to appoint attorneys, licence in mortmain, and so on. Out of these hundreds of petitions the great majority are concerned with judicial or quasi-judicial matters. And then let us notice that, when the knights and burgesses complained in the Easter parliament of 1309 that receivers of petitions had not been appointed, they described the nature of the petitions they had in mind: those concerning the wrongs (tortz) and grievances which could not be redressed by the common law nor in any other manner without special warrant. Are we mistaken in saying that they are describing, in the language of the early fourteenth century, petitions concerned with judicial or quasi-judicial matters? The knights and burgesses were certainly not concerned on this occasion with petitions for special favours, petitions that might be presented at any time, but with such petitions as comprised the great majority of those presented in 1305. It might be argued — as is constantly argued in the High Court today, for the dividing line is very uncertain — that the replies to some of the petitions presented in 1305, though they touched the operation of the law, involved administrative rather than judicial action; but whittle down the judicial element as we may, we are confronted with a mass, the majority, of petitions which ask for justice. Nor were the Lords Committees or Stubbs in error when they recognised in the early rolls of parliament the records of judicial sessions of the king's court, however wrong their classification of those sessions might be. We do not need the mantle of Maitland to legitimate our own conclusions, when we have the corroboration of *Fleta* and the *Ordinances;* but it may be of interest to cite his conclusion on the nature of the parliament he was studying:

A new tribunal is evolved, or rather, two tribunals become three. We can see this development taking place in the pages of Bracton and Fleta. Bracton knows but two of those courts of which we are speaking: there are justices resident at the bench; there are yet more exalted justices attending the king's person. Fleta knows three: there are justices resident at the bench; there are other justices who fill the king's own place, but above even them there is another tribunal, "for the king has his court in his council in his parliaments. . . ."

At this point it seems desirable to attempt to clarify the position of the petitioner in parliament and to explain why parliamentary petitions have from very early times been placed in a class apart. It is to be remembered that, though parliament was, as Maitland said, a court, it was a very special kind of court. Over many centuries its sessions were, for the most part, irregular and there might be long intervals between one parliament and another, despite the attempts made from time to time to induce some ordered periodicity. In face of this difference between parliament and the ordinary courts of common law and equity, with their regular law terms, it may seem open to question whether petitioners to the king in council in parliament had a right to petition and to be answered in the same sense as a plaintiff in a court of common law had a right to writ and judgment or a plaintiff in a court of equity had a right to petition and decree. The procedure in all three cases differed widely. In parliament the king invited petitioners to deliver their petitions to the receivers at a certain time and place. He appointed triers or auditors to determine the answer or, where they felt unable to do so, to refer them to the great council. If this was a new departure under Edward I, the procedure must have had its origin very early in his reign, and while Edward modified the procedure, he did not initiate a new approach to the king; he regulated a flood of petitions that threatened to become unmanageable. This flood was a new phenomenon; but already when Edward became king, the petition, the plaint, oral or in writing, had a very long history in the king's courts. How should it have been otherwise, for the king is the fountain of justice? "This is the reason," says Bracton, "why the king has been created and elected: that he may do justice to every man." And were there not some famous words written well before Bracton's time: *nulli negabimus aut differemus rectum et justiciam* [to no one will we deny or delay right and justice]?

It is indisputable therefore that the subject had a right to petition the king, and the king invited him to exercise that right in parliament and, by implication, gave him a right to an answer. But this right was not an enforceable right: a right cannot be enforced against the king. The king might, indeed, fail to appoint receivers of petitions, though, if this happened on occasion, the failure seems to have been repaired as soon as possible after complaint had been made. . . . The right to petition and to be answered in parliament was therefore a qualified right, a right that diminished in importance in the course of Edward III's reign and still further as the Middle Ages waned, though it does not seem that this was of serious disadvantage to the subject, who found in the Court of Chancery an ampler measure of relief than he was wont to find in parliament.

This is not, of course, the whole story. In view of the importance that is usually attached to the part played by the commons in parliament some few words should be spared for them. They, too, as a body had the right to petition the king. It was the accepted doctrine in 1399 that the knights of the shire, at least, had the right to expose the grievances of the people and to sue for suitable remedies. The commons were perhaps more certain of a reply to their petitions than the private petitioner. To a complaint by the commons in 1339 that a full reply had not been given to all petitions and to a request that replies should be returned before parliament rose, the king answered that replies had been given to every petition presented by the commons in former parliaments before those parliaments had been dissolved and that, as regards private petitions presented in the parliament then in session, it was his wish that the auditors should determine them before they departed. But though the commons might have some advantage in this respect and though, as we have seen, they came to play a part in the expediting of private petitions, any right they had was qualified. The medieval king was unable to shake off the peers, for, as a lawyer writing under Henry VI said, "the king is intrinsicate within his council and may not do without them"; but he was able to rule without summoning parliament, without the assistance of the commons. There was no one to compel him to hold a parliament, and it is by no means certain that the rarity of parliaments and the consequent cessation of common petitions were resented by the country at large. . . .

It is no longer disputed, as it was by Stubbs, that the dispensing of justice was a function of parliament; but objection is still taken to our statement that the essence of parliament — we spoke with particular reference to the parliaments of Edward I and Edward II — is the dispensing of justice. It may have been a mistake on our part to use a metaphor. "Essence" we have been reminded, as the word is used by philosophers and theologians, is that which constitutes the being of a thing. But on this occasion, as the context showed, we were speaking not as metaphysicians but as historians; and had it occurred to us that there was doubt as to our meaning, we might have used another phrase or explained that "essence" had here the ordinary meaning of "distinctive quality"; the quality which arrested the attention of the author of *Fleta* and the Ordainers; the quality without which there would have been no volume one of the Rolls of Parliament nor other printed texts that supplement it. The facts are not really in dispute. The one constant attribute of parliament, so far as our evidence goes, was, for the better part of a century, the hearing of private petitions, petitions which in most instances asked for justice. But that is not the sole evidence for the judicial function of parliament. To give but three examples: the statute called Rageman provided that offenders should be brought before the king in parliament; the Statute of Winchester required the justices to report to the king in parliament breaches of the provisions for maintaining the peace; special commissioners were appointed in 1309 to hear complaints of tortious prises and to bring those guilty before the council in parliament. We could add much more evidence of a like kind.

As, we believe, we were the first to demonstrate, business in great variety came before parliament in its earlier years. Nor would there seem to be any reason why any matter that might come before the king's council should not come before the king in council in parliament, if this were a suitable occasion. We have at no time suggested that, because the distinctive quality of parliament was the dispensing of justice, this was its sole purpose, though we have emphasised, and rightly emphasised, the unique importance of this function in face of the denial by Stubbs that parliament, in the true sense, as he conceived it, had such a function at all. If his doctrine — the doctrine that parliament is a "national council," "the concentration of the three estates" — had been historically valid, then the king's council, which dispensed justice, would have stood outside parliament, and Maitland's suggestion (for he professed to go no further) that "a session of the king's council is the core and essence of every *parliamentum*" would have been absurd. In truth, it is Stubbs's doctrine that is unwarrantable, and no one would venture to defend it; but there is still, it would seem, great reluctance to abandon the inferences that proceeded from it. The imaginary parliament of Stubbs, or something very like it, has been denominated the "representative parliament" in contradistinction to the "pre-representative parliament," and we have been presented afresh with a picture, made familiar in another guise by Stubbs and Pollard, of a plurality of parliaments. The dichotomy seems, in any case, to be false, since it suggests that there was a point of time at which "pre-representative parliaments" ceased and "representative parliaments" began. If, however, we take our starting point in 1258 and continue to 1327, we find that, over a period little short of seventy years, parliaments to which representatives of shires or towns were summoned, for one purpose or another, alternated with parliaments to which there was no such summons. Parliaments of the latter type predominated, it is true, until the year 1300 and parliaments of the former type thereafter; but there is no "pre" or "post." "Pre-representative" and "representative" parliaments co-existed. There were not two kinds of parliament, though in some there was business for which it was deemed desirable to summon representatives of the "commons"; but, as Pollard said, "they probably took a less active part in parliament than the audience does in a public meeting of today."

The true dividing line is 1327. From 1327 onwards all parliaments included representatives of the shires and boroughs. The intention behind this development was doubtless political, but, as we have explained, a significant change had taken place. The emergence of the doctrine of peerage meant that the barons could no longer be petitioners, no longer speak as the mouthpiece of the *commune*. In 1306 the knights of the shire could form one body with the barons. In 1327, although they are still quite distinct from the burgesses, the knights act in common with them: a step has been taken which will in process of time give parliament a house of commons. During the reign of Edward II there had been wrought, unwittingly and without foresight, a great constitutional change. The significance of this change may not at first have been appreciated, but before long Bishop Granson of Exeter could put the position in a striking metaphor. "By its nature the substance of the Crown lies primarily in the king's person, as head, and in the peers of the land, as members . . . and in this way the Crown is so conditioned that there cannot be severance without dividing the kingship." As was said a century or so later, "the king is intrinsicate within his council." If, on the other hand, the doctrine of peerage was significant in giving the representatives of shires and boroughs a constant and con-

tinuous function in parliament, that of presenting common petitions, it was equally significant in giving a constitution to the council, whether in parliament or out of parliament. There was, however, no sudden or marked breach with the past. Bishops, earls and barons had hitherto been present in the council with judges and ministers; but henceforward the status, as well as the number, of the king's servants in the council was to decline while the status of the peers was to be exalted.

Though the constitution of the council might change, its dominance in parliament was undiminished. Obviously the work done by the council in parliament varied with the business brought before parliament. Prior to 1327, taking one parliament with another, business other than judicial can have occupied relatively little time. We should perhaps emphasise that whatever business was transacted in parliament was council business, and though the majority of petitions were disposed of by a small body of triers and never reached the great council, all were, as the king said in 1309, "delivres par son conseil" [delivered by his council]. We may think, with Stubbs, that such business was unimportant; and it may well be that in the eyes of the council the dominant interest in some parliaments was not the highly personal and largely routine answering of petitions but the issue of war or peace or taxation or legislation, though, even so, there is no need to postulate large assemblies on these occasions or anxious debates. Such matters came before parliament because it was convenient that they should be discussed then, not because it was imperative that they should be determined only in parliament. They might equally be discussed by the council elsewhere than in parliament, and the principle that parliament was the proper occasion for their discussion was hardly established before the fifteenth century. The issue whether to go to war or not came before a great council in 1401, and it is clear from the council minute that it was uncertain whether the assent of parliament was necessary, though the balance of opinion seems to have lain in that direction. In the previous year, a great council had decided to avoid calling a parliament, which would have been necessary if the "common people" were to be taxed, but it had been resolved that the lords spiritual and temporal should grant an aid. In Ireland in the fourteenth and fifteenth centuries there was no questioning the competence of a great council to decide that a general tax should be levied; and the difference between English and Irish practice seems not to lie in the lesser authority of a great council in England but to arise from the long exclusion of the commons from English great councils. Whether a statute could be made elsewhere than in parliament seems still to have been an open issue in 1353. The attitude taken by the commons towards legislation in great councils ensured that statutes were henceforth made in parliament; but so far as we can judge, this was a new development, quite unexpected by the government. When, therefore, it is said that parliament is omnicompetent, it should be added that this is because the king in council is omnicompetent. Whether the council sits in parliament or not is a matter for the king's discretion, although gradually conventions arise which limit the exercise of his discretion.

We cannot, as Stubbs seems to have done, approach the question of the functions of parliament a priori. What those functions were must be decided on evidence, by the simple method of enumeration. But we must take precautions lest we give undue weight to some part of the evidence. . . .

We have been an unconscionable time making an end, but since last we wrote of the English parliament many things have been said which invited comment. Let these be our last words. The discussion of the nature and characteristics of parliament under Henry III and the first three Edwards threatens to become a vain dispute about the niceties of language. In such disputes we have no interest. Our concern is with historical realities, with what was done and said in the thirteenth and fourteenth centuries. So long as these are described in sufficient fullness and with sufficient accuracy, it matters little what terms are used, provided the terms are reasonably unambiguous and fitting to the century to which they are applied. But we confess that, just as we deprecate the selection of evidence to support some preconceived conclusion, so we wince at such phrases as "political assembly" or "representative parliament," which have a meaning at the present day that is not apposite to the reigns of Henry III and the first two Edwards, not even to those few parliaments where "politics" may be discerned in the clashes between the king and a baronial opposition. "In his parliaments the king in council holds his court in the presence of prelates, earls, barons, nobles and others learned in the law." What have "politics," what has "representation," to do with these parliaments?

# High Politics in Parliament

## BERTIE WILKINSON

Bertie Wilkinson (1898–   ) studied at Manchester and has taught at the University of Toronto since 1938. He has published *The Chancery under Edward III* (1929), *Studies in the Constitutional History of the Thirteenth and Fourteenth Centuries* (1937), and the three-volume *Constitutional History of Medieval England* (1948–1958), from which the selection below is taken. In these works Wilkinson is an outspoken critic of the Maitland-McIlwain approach to parliamentary origins, projecting in its place the picture of a vigorous political assembly, similar to the assembly described by Stubbs.

IT IS ALMOST A TRUISM to state that there has never been a greater need than at the present time for a lively common attack on the problems of the medieval constitution. It will need all the combined efforts of the scholars who are primarily devoted to this subject to keep it, matchless in its intrinsic significance and matchless in its methods and traditions of scholarship, in that place in contemporary historical interest which it deserves. The constitutional history of medieval England has, indeed, never been more significant as a subject of study, or more interesting. It is in a fascinating period of transition, when the certainties and systems of Stubbs and Maitland are dissolving but when nothing equally authoritative and comprehensive has been produced to take their place. It is a measure of the greatness of these historians that they have held sway for so long over succeeding generations; but nothing is more certain than that these generations will sooner or later have to make an interpretation of the great truths of past constitutional development for themselves. There can be no finality in history; and the kind of history which captures a generation will always be that which helps it to an understanding of its own problems and inner sources of strength. Nor, perhaps, will any period of history be more significant for this understanding than the late medieval period of formation, when the nations of Europe first combined order and liberty within the framework of the modern state. . . .

Even in the cautious pages of Stubbs, G. T. Lapsley wrote, the works of the fourteenth-century parliaments (and presumably of the thirteenth) are often exhibited in the light reflected from the seventeenth century. Later writers, he observed with apparent approval, have departed strongly and properly from this view, and the tendency now is to minimize the importance of parliament and to bring forward the council and administrative machinery as dominating the constitutional struggle of the period. Against this latest tendency, however, it is possible to suggest that in relation to parliament, at least, historians may have departed too strongly from the views of Bishop Stubbs. It is true that Stubbs read too many notions derived from the seventeenth century into the fourteenth; yet he may be accused of underestimating rather than exaggerating the parliamentary radicalism of the earlier period; and there are very good arguments which may be adduced to defend the central position which he gave to parliament

From Bertie Wilkinson, *The Constitutional History of Medieval England, 1216–1399, with Select Documents,* 3 volumes (Toronto, 1948–1958), III, vii, pp. 265–273, 280–284, 295. Reprinted by permission of Longmans, Green & Co. Ltd. and of Barnes & Noble, Inc.

in the constitutional struggles of that age.

The essence of parliament in the Stubbsian tradition was that of a great political assembly, the "forum of the nation," in which according to a tradition of the greatest antiquity the king and his subjects foregathered to dispose of the nation's affairs. Since Stubbs, there have developed a multiplicity of views all departing more or less from this simple monolithic concept, and testifying by their variations to the vigour of recent thinking on this important point. The school of writers which has departed farthest from Stubbs is that which derives ultimately from his younger and some think even greater contemporary, F. W. Maitland. The departure, which was at first expressed in gentle and far from challenging terms, has since led to a wide cleavage of opinion. Instead of regarding parliament as being essentially a political assembly, the disciples of Maitland have regarded it as essentially a court of justice. Its history is to be explained in terms of this inner nature, as are its functions and personnel at various stages in the medieval period. The only essential part of the assembly was the council; its only indispensable function was the judicial work of the conciliar body. The decisive turning-point in its history was not the addition of representative estates, which were never completely necessary to its full existence during the medieval period (though custom tended to make them so), but the transformation of the early political gatherings into judicial and conciliar assemblies. This occurred, it is believed, roughly at the time of the Provisions of Oxford; by the reign of Edward I, parliament was a court placed above other courts and devised to dispense the highest justice in the land. According to this interpretation parliament served an altogether different and more limited purpose than that which had been claimed for it in the pages of Bishop Stubbs.

The consequences which flow from this fundamental divergence between the "schools" of Maitland and Stubbs extend to almost every problem of the medieval parliament; from its origin to its composition, from its relation to the monarch to its evolution into the High Court of the Realm. One view tends to make parliament the instrument of the ruler; the other makes it essentially a meeting between the king and the *universitas,* serving the purpose of both. There are many concepts of parliament which lie between these extremes. Some of these, for example, reject the notion that parliament was essentially a court, but nevertheless hold that it was a "conciliar" assembly. Sometimes it may be suspected that such compromises entail the combination of incompatible elements; and it seems probable that historians will have to make a choice between the two main lines of interpretation which cannot be reconciled. According to one, parliament was a political assembly; according to the other, it was a body whose essence is to be found in the judicial functions which it exercised in common with the council, and which expanded in due course into those of the High Court of the Realm.

Of the sources which throw light on this problem, the most obvious are the Rolls of Parliament. Unfortunately, they only begin in the reign of Edward I. At that time, they consist almost exclusively of a record of judicial proceedings — the unsystematic recordings of the activities of a court. The haphazard arrangement and fragmentary character of the records appear, not as something to be explained away, but rather as something to be expected from a body whose business mostly originated in written petitions to the king. Like the rolls of any court of law, those of parliament were at first merely a "putting together of odds and ends." . . . It must be emphasized, however, that no historian can properly deny their judicial nature. . . . It is only the conclusions which are to be drawn from them which are a matter of debate.

Despite the character of the early Rolls, it may still be doubted whether the activities they reflect provided the essential reason why parliament was summoned. Of course the different people who attended had different reasons for placing a high value upon it. Those who put forward petitions probably cherished their access to king and council; but petitions to the king could be made at any time, and did not need a session of parliament. Moreover, it seems likely that anybody, whether summoned to parliament or not, could petition the king during a parliamentary assembly. These facts seem to suggest that the judicial work which took place there, derived from petitions, was incidental. The main purpose for which "members" were summoned, and which was peculiar to them, was the weighty business of the realm and of foreign lands, referred to by Edward I in 1280. Finally, and this is of great importance, we know that in the early parliaments much political business was transacted which was never, or very rarely, recorded on the rolls of the parliaments of Edward I. The parliament of Edward I was becoming an institution with an entity and traditions of its own; but it had not developed so far as to have a record of its "corporate" activities, distinct from those of the king and council who acted in the assembly of parliament or who acted, as *Fleta* put it, in the presence of the magnates. It was the king and council in parliament who judged and heard petitions in the age of *Fleta*, not the High Court of Parliament.

Two other major sources of our knowledge of parliament before the death of Edward I are the chronicles, which contain frequent and important references to particular assemblies, and the writs of summons [omitted in the selection reprinted below] which often indicate briefly the purpose for which individuals or representatives were commanded to attend. The former were no doubt inconsistent and lacking in precision in their references to parliament; and the latter probably tended to become conventional; but together they represent a formidable body of evidence. They tell us what purpose was seen in the actual assemblies by the educated opinion of the age, and also what the king and his ministers proclaimed to be the purpose of the parliamentary assembly. Matthew Paris in particular wrote in great detail and with a sensitive ear for significant formulae, and he has left a fine memorial to some of the great public assemblies which occurred between 1232 and 1258.

The first conclusion suggested by these documents is that the general concern of the early parliaments was with what we may call politics. The second is that the general assemblies which were summoned after 1242 were as much genuine parliaments as those which were later summoned by Edward I. The third, which will, indeed, only become fully apparent at a later stage, is that there was no real break in the early development of the parliamentary assembly. It follows from all this that parliament was already well established, and its problems were already very familiar, long before the end of the thirteenth century. The fourth and final conclusion is that there was a deep distinction between the council and parliament. In particular, the two bodies were summoned for different purposes, or at least in a different relationship to the king.

The last conclusion need not be further debated, though perhaps one fleeting reference should again be made to the Provisions of Oxford, where the council, though plainly exceptional in its attributes, was no less plainly distinguished from parliament whose essence was the community of the realm. One or two comments should be offered, however, on the great "public assemblies" of this age, now first coming to be called parliaments, and on one or two of the summonses which help us to understand their nature and the footing on which the knights first made there the tentative and uncertain beginning of what was destined to be a glorious career.

The gathering of 1237 was not called a parliament but it was summoned by a writ which closely resembled those used in connection with the parliamentary assemblies of Edward I. The earls and barons were gathered together to treat about royal business which concerned the whole realm. According to the king, the prelates and magnates had treaty with him concerning the state of the ruler and of the kingdom. It is quite certain that this formula was considered to be significant. The assembly of 1237 was, in fact, a meeting between the king and the *universitas;* its concern was the welfare of the *regnum;* and it shows a distinction between the magnates and the council, composed of the *secretarii,* one of whom acted as "meditator between the king and the magnates of the realm."

The assembly of 1242 produced what Stubbs called the first authorized account of a parliamentary debate. Matthew Paris both gave his own account and reproduced a record which had been drawn up, he said, lest the replies of the barons should be forgotten. The magnates were summoned, he said, to hear the wish of the king and the business for which he had called them. He did not record the terms of the writ, perhaps because they were not so striking; but we have the enrolment of the actual summons, maybe the first such to survive; and it strongly resembles the corresponding writs of Edward I's reign. Henry wanted the magnates to treat with him and with each other concerning arduous business of his foreign policy which especially touched the estate of his realm. The money which the king asked for was to be spent for the advantage of the king and the kingdom. It was thus for business which was both general and political, at least as far as this kind of evidence will take us, that parliament was summoned in 1242.

In 1254, the surviving writs summoning assemblies began to include those directed to the shires commanding the attendance of "representative" knights. The problem of the relationship of the Commons to parliament begins to be important; and enough writs have survived to suggest

that this was the case even before the accession of Edward I. We do not yet understand, and maybe shall never quite understand, all the implications of the carefully worded summons of knights in 1254 . . . to be before a meeting of the council in the king's absence. The knights were not summoned to say "yes" or "no" to a request for aid to the king, but to say "what sort of aid they will give." But we should notice their summons on these terms was suggested by the magnates in England rather than by Henry overseas; and it was probably a recognition that the voice of the knights was something which, in regard to taxation or military service, could not be safely ignored.

Important summonses of knights and burgesses to parliament . . . were issued in the period of baronial control and experiment between 1258 and 1265. The magnates, who were controlling the king, summoned the knights in 1261 to "treat" about the common affairs of the kingdom, apparently on terms of equality with the magnates; but the king, who was at odds with his nobles, issued a countersummons in which he invited the knights merely to have a colloquy and to understand his honourable intentions. This seems to indicate that the significance of the terms of summons was well understood.

In the famous Montfortian parliament of June 1264, unmistakably expressing baronial and not royal views of such matters, knights were summoned to "treat" about the affairs of both the king and the kingdom, and it is possible but not certain that both knights and burgesses received a similar summons in January 1265.

Thus parliament was already well established by the age of Edward I, and the question of enlarging the *universitas* there had already arisen. If parliament was still an occasion or an event, it was rapidly clothing itself with the forms and procedures of an institution. The political activities of the earlier period continued to be fundamental. Justice soon began to overshadow other matters; but Edward I himself disapproved of this; he wanted to keep his hands free for the great business of his realm and of his "foreines" lands. The English parliament was a European phenomenon, the product of European conditions of political life; and it was marked by universal characteristics. "It is the custom" Humbert de Romans, Master General of the Dominican Order, wrote about the time of Edward I's accession,

for great kings to hold parliaments at appointed times every year, at which assemble many counsellors and many of the worldly great and many prelates. These parliaments are held for three great purposes: that the more important public affairs may be the more wisely resolved there after more searching considerations; that account may be rendered there by the ministers of the realm; and that order may be taken there for the good government of the realm.

It is far more important to insist on the implications of such a description than on the many meanings of *parliamentum,* or the extent to which parliament was still not an institution but an event. . . .

Some clues as to the nature of parliament under Edward I, and as to the king's policy towards it, are likely to be provided by the writs of summons to the assembly. Stubbs made very good use of these writs, as have some modern historians, notably J. G. Edwards; but their significance has been denied or ignored by some important researchers. There is, however, positive evidence as to the existence of a "parliamentary writ," and there are strong general grounds for expecting its wording to be significant. On the whole, the writs of summons to parliament do, indeed, seem to throw a flood of light on the nature of the assembly.

As far as this evidence will take us. there was no revolution in the parliamentary assembly between the days of Henry III and of Edward I. Parliament met to dispose of business of common interest to the king and his subjects which might be both judicial and political. The purpose

for which the magnates came was to "treat." They did not come primarily to petition or seek remedy for judicial wrongs, when their position was, like that of any other subject, one of supplicating, rather than of "treating."

The writs of summons to the knights and burgesses, . . . were much more variable; and they cannot be accused of adherence to any one formula. There is hardly a doubt that their variations reflect changes in the royal policy. The representatives of the towns and shires had no claim to be put alongside the magnates in parliament; but they had a claim to be consulted when their interests were directly involved; and this was probably recognized even after the royalist victories of 1265 and 1266. It may be that the desirability of their consent to taxation explains their summons to attend the assemblies of 1268 and of April and October 1275. In any case, the last two writs have much in common with those of 1264 and (probably) 1265. But between then and November 1295, the king summoned knights or knights and burgesses only to hear and do the things shown to them, or to give counsel and to consent to matters already agreed upon. In both July 1290 and November 1294, the knights were summoned to attend when the king and magnates had already made their most important decisions; indeed, the wording of the writs makes it possible that the main reason for their summons was merely that they might bind their constituents. There may have been another reason. In 1290 the magnates probably showed a clear unwillingness to bind the commons in their absence. They voted a grant only as far as in them lay. In 1294, it has been conjectured, the lords declined to come to a final decision until representatives of the shires had been consulted.

There was probably some difference of opinion between the king and his magnates as to the wording of such writs; and it is likely that the latter rather than the former wished the participation of the Commons to be enlarged. It is true that it was apparently the monarch himself who gave the Commons a place alongside the Lords in 1295. This was the occasion of Stubbs's famous "model" parliament, and both knights and citizens were summoned with full power to do what should be ordained by common council, by implication "treating" alongside the magnates with the king. Such a writ of summons was to be used for the next six centuries, with the addition of the word "consent" under Edward II. It did not bind the representatives simply to do what should be shown on the king's behalf, or things agreed upon beforehand by the magnates. The king's lawyers, it has been said, took the idea of the common will of the communities of the shire and town one step farther, and enlarged it into the idea of the community of the realm, the community of England which transcended all other communities. Thus common counsel provided the will of all the realm; the practical problem of consent was solved; and the venerable maxim *Quod omnes tangit* was literally and legally fulfilled.

There is certainly much truth in all this; but perhaps it is a little too favourable to the king. The immediate problem of 1295 was probably caused by the summons not of the lower laity but of the lower clergy. The latter were jealous of their privileges in Convocation, as may be seen very clearly by the twin summonses of 1283. . . . In 1294, the clergy were summoned alongside the laity; in 1295, they were summoned as integral members of parliament, to share the common burden of national defence. It was probably the devising of formulae to express these purposes which caused the king's advisers to "liberalize" the summonses to the burgesses and knights. Even then, Edward did not concede to the lay Commons the same power to "treat, ordain and do" along with other members of the assembly, which he accorded to the clergy and barons.

The summons of 1295 may have reflected a liberalizing of Edward's policy towards the knights and burgesses; but it showed an extension of his claims towards the clergy which helped to provoke the bull *Clericis Laicos* of Boniface VIII. The writs of 1295 hardly serve to show Edward as an architect of parliament in the Stubbsian sense; but they do show the importance attached both to the attendance of the Commons and to the wording of the parliamentary writ of summons. Whatever the intentions of the king, the writs were in fact a landmark in the development of the Commons in parliament. They did not attend regularly even after 1295, but they attended more and more frequently; and they achieved an important recognition of both their powers derived from their constituents and their position in the parliamentary assembly, partaking in however ambiguous a manner in the common counsel of the realm.

Thus, we may perhaps conclude, the Edwardian parliament of the writs was an assembly where the king and the magnates acted by common counsel, treating together about the affairs of the king and the kingdom, the affairs common to both. It was an assembly in which the Commons were gradually establishing a secure foothold, despite the reluctance of the ruler, on terms more liberal than those whose essence was simply loyalty and obedience to the king. This was after all nothing more than the logical outcome of the new position of the knights and burgesses in the national order; but it was nevertheless something they might never have attained had it not been for the opposition of magnates and clergy to the policy of the king. . . . In all this, we may almost certainly see the workings of a great political assembly which far transcended in both its scope and in its significance the limitations of a council or a court.

# Omnicompetence: Justice and Politics in Parliament

## SIR JOHN GORONWY EDWARDS

Sir John Goronwy Edwards (1891–    ) has taught at Oxford and the University of London, where he is now Professor Emeritus. He is a past president of the Royal Historical Society and past editor of the *English Historical Review*. In a number of periodical articles, Edwards has investigated the functions of early parliaments and measured the participation and influence of representatives in those assemblies. The selection below, taken from the Twenty-Second Annual David Murray Lecture, which he delivered at Glasgow University in 1955, describes early parliaments as "omnicompetent," or capable of handling business in both political and judicial areas.

IT IS DURING the twelve-forties that we first hear in England of a political institution called "parliament." We begin to hear of it at that time, under that name, both in the chronicles and in the records of the central government — in the records, for instance, of the chancery. That this parliament, when it first appeared, contained no representatives, was one of the basic conclusions established by the pioneer work of Prynne.[1] But there remained a further question. What was the nature of this pre-representative parliament? What was its essence as an institution? What was the essential element in its *composition*; and what was the essential element in its *functions*? In other words, who must be members of it, and what functions must be performed in it, before it could rightly be denominated by the term "parliament"?

This question did not for some time attract much attention: in that specific form, indeed, it was not perhaps even broached until as late as 1893. In that year Maitland published in the Rolls Series an edition of the parliament roll of 1305. To it he prefaced a weighty introduction in which,

among other things, he pointedly discussed this very question of the institutional essence of the early parliament. That discussion is now regarded as a turning-point in the study of the medieval English parliament. Yet Maitland himself summed up his discussion in words that seem rather tentative. He said:

> It seemed necessary to remind readers who are conversant with the "parliaments" of later days, that about the parliaments of Edward I's time there is still much to be discovered, and that should they come to the opinion that a session of the king's council is the core and essence of every *parliamentum* . . . they will not be departing very far from the path marked out by books that are already classical.

. . . We may note that subsequent discussion since Maitland's day has suggested the desirability of modifying just one word in his proposition that "a session of the king's council was the core and essence of every parliament." It is the word "essence." The phrase "core and essence" was a very apt one to express the place of the king's council in parliament, provided that the word "essence" was taken in its broader sense of "the most important constituent element of anything." But "essence" also

[1] William Prynne, *A Brief Register, Kalendar and Survey of the Several Kinds and Forms of All Parliamentary Writs,* 4 volumes (London, 1659–1664). [Editor's note.]

From Sir J. G. Edwards, *Historians and the Medieval English Parliament* (Glasgow, 1960), pp. 8–9, 12–23. Reprinted by permission of Jackson, Son and Company and of the author.

has a strict meaning, and in its strict meaning it has been made momentous by philosophers and theologians. In that strict sense, the "essence" of anything is that which constitutes its being, that which makes it what it is—in the case before us, that which makes a parliament a parliament. In that sense we may not say that "a session of the king's council was the core *and essence* of every parliament." The evidence indicates that in the strict sense the "essence" of parliament in composition was that it was *the king's council afforced,* i.e. the king's continual council plus others. The council *plus*: that was in the strict sense the "essence" of parliament in composition. The afforcement, the *plus,* as well as the council, was equally "of the essence" so far as the composition of parliament was concerned.

As regards the functions of parliament, the general trend of scholarship during the last thirty or forty years has been, on the whole, to lay increasing stress upon the "judicial" functions performed in the earlier parliaments, and especially in the pre-representative parliaments. This trend has been illustrated, though in markedly varying degrees, in the works of a number of scholars. Here again, much of the impetus has come ultimately from Maitland's introduction to the *Memoranda de Parliamento*—though here too, in turn, the way for that Introduction had been prepared by the *Report* of the Lords' Committee. It is true to say, however, that what is now the most familiar form of the doctrine about the "judicial" functions performed in early parliaments is, in at least one very important respect, much more extreme than anything stated or implied in Maitland's measured discussion of the subject in the *Memoranda de Parliamento.* Maitland undoubtedly gave great prominence there to the "judicial" business transacted in parliament — he was bound to do so, if only because it bulked so large in the particular parliament roll that he was editing — but he neither said nor implied

that this "judicial" business had some unique significance which distinguished it from the other kinds of business transacted in parliament. That, however, is precisely what has been asserted — with marked emphasis and sustained iteration — in the doctrine that has subsequently become current. Because these "judicial" functions seem to have been exercised in all (or nearly all) of the earlier parliaments, whereas other functions — deliberative or legislative or taxative — were exercised only in some of those parliaments, it has been inferred that the "judicial" functions which were exercised in all parliaments were the functions that constituted "the essence of parliament," or in other words, were the functions whose exercise made a parliament a parliament; whereas the seemingly more occasional functions which were exercised only in some of the parliaments were "non-essential." These latter functions, it has therefore been concluded, should be "stripped away" when we come as historians to decide what in essence the pre-representative parliaments were: according to the doctrine, "the essence of them was the dispensing of justice." Or alternatively, according to a less extreme form of the doctrine, parliament was "primarily a court of justice," and "its earliest function was judicial."

That "judicial" functions of great number and importance were performed in parliament, particularly in its pre-representative phase, but also (though decreasingly) after it had become representative, has been known since Prynne's day, and has never been denied. These "judicial" functions were exercised partly in determining cases civil and criminal which either came into parliament as a court of first instance, or were adjourned into parliament by inferior courts. But the "judicial" functions which have attracted special attention are those which were performed in parliament in connection with petitions. These petitions came to the king in parliament often in considerable numbers. They were concerned with a great variety of matters, but were all alike in one respect: they all asked that the king *of his grace* would provide the petitioners with a remedy for this or that grievance or difficulty. In some cases, the provision of a remedy would involve action that was really "judicial," especially if the petitioner happened to complain, as petitioners not infrequently did, that proceedings in which he was involved had come to a stand in some lower court owing to doubts or disagreements among the judges: in such cases the king in parliament could, if he thought fit, give a ruling or instruction which might resolve the doubt or disagreement, and get the court concerned moving again. In such cases, which quite commonly arose out of petitions, the king in parliament would be doing grace to the petitioner by performing what was a judicial or quasi-judicial act. But in the case of many other petitions, the king in parliament could and did do grace to the petitioner without any action that was "judicial," i.e. without any action that involved a decision on a matter of law. This is a material point, because there has been a tacit but misleading tendency to treat all petitioning in parliament as though it was necessarily and essentially "judicial." In actual fact, petitions by no means always asked for "justice," i.e. for action that was judicial: many of them (as Maitland duly emphasized) asked for pure favours. What all petitions did ask for was "grace." The audience of petitions in parliament, therefore, always involved the dispensing of grace, but by no means always the dispensing of "justice." So we must beware of exaggerating the amount of "judicial" work that was involved in disposing of petitions in parliament.

But even if all petitions expedited in parliament had involved action that could rightly be called "judicial," there would still be objections to the doctrine that "the essence of parliaments is the dispensing of justice," and that the other functions performed in parliaments may be "stripped away" as "non-essentials." The objections are raised by two familiar but important documents, dating respectively from 1258 and 1280, and belonging therefore to the pre-representative period of parliament.

1. Included in the provisions of Oxford of 1258 are the following clauses:

Il fet a remembrer ke les xxiv unt ordene ke treis parlemenz seient par an. Le premerein as utaves de Sein Michel: le secund le demein de la Chandelur: le terz le premer jor de June, ceo est a saver, treis semeines devant le Seint John. A ces treis parlemenz, vendrunt les cunseillers le rei esluz, tut ne seint il pas mandez, pur ver le estat del reaume et pur treter les cummuns bosoingnes del reaume et del rei ensement. E autre fez ensement quant mester serra per le mandement le rei.

Si fet a remembre ke le commun eslise xii prodes homes, ke vendrunt as parlemenz et autre fez quant mester serra, quant le rei u sun cunseil les mandera pur treter de bosoingnes le rei et del reaume. E ke le commun tendra pur estable ceo ke ces xii frunt. E ceo serra fet pur esparnier le cust del commun.

[It should be remembered that the twenty-four have ordained that there are to be three parliaments a year: the first on the octave of St. Michael, the second on the morrow of Candlemas, and the third on the first day of June, that is to say, three weeks before [the feast of] St. John. To these three parliaments the chosen councillors of the king shall come, even if they are not summoned, in order to examine the state of the kingdom and to consider the common needs of the kingdom and likewise of the king; and by the king's command [they shall come] also at other times, whenever it is necessary.

So too it should be remembered that the community is to elect twelve good men, who shall come to the three parliaments at other times, when there is need and when the king and his council summon them to consider the affairs of the king and kingdom. And [it has been decided] that the community shall hold as established whatever these twelve shall do. And this is to reduce the cost to the community.]²

It will be seen that these clauses provide for a "parliament," which is described as consisting of the continual council afforced (so as to save expense) by twelve "prodes homes" who would act on behalf of the whole "community." This parliament is to meet in each year on three specified dates, 6 October, 3 February and 1 June; in other words, at three equal — and as nearly as possible *exactly equal* — intervals of 17 weeks, 17 weeks and 18 weeks. On those three occasions the parliaments are to meet even if not summoned: hence the prescribing of precise dates, so that the persons concerned will know when to assemble even if no summons comes. Parliament, it is provided, can also meet on other occasions besides the three specified, if need arise, but for those meetings a summons will naturally be necessary.

Now there is general agreement among historians that the English parliament in its pre-representative form consisted of the king's continual council afforced by "prodes homes" [good men] of various kinds, and that it met several times a year at more or less regular intervals, and also at other times when required. The passage that has just been cited from the Provisions of Oxford happens to be the earliest extant description of those periodically-recurring pre-representative parliaments. What it says about their function is therefore especially noteworthy. It describes their business twice, in the following terms:

(a) "pur ver le estat del reaume et pur treter les communs bosoingnes del reaume et del rei ensement" [in order to examine the state of the kingdom and to consider

the common needs of the kingdom and likewise of the king];

(b) "pur treter de bosoingnes le rei et del reaume" [to consider the affairs of the king and kingdom].

If words mean anything, those terms are much wider than the dispensing of "justice." They may well include it, but the dispensing of "justice" was but one aspect of the "common business of the kingdom": other aspects also would have to be dealt with by the recurring parliaments if they were adequately to achieve their function of "viewing the state of the kingdom and treating the common business of the kingdom and of the king." And that conclusion is corroborated in a very striking way by our second document.

2. This document belongs to the year 1280, and is particularly relevant because it happens to deal specifically with the subject of petitions in parliament, and we have already seen that it was precisely these petitions that occasioned much of the "judicial" and quasi-judicial work that was performed in parliament. On the subject with which it deals, no document could be better-informed or more authoritative, for it was drawn up in the chancery, and it is enrolled for record in the Close Roll of the eighth year of King Edward I. It runs thus:

Pur ceo ke la gent ke venent al parlement le roy sunt sovent deslaez et desturbez a grant grevance de eus et de la curt par la multitudine des peticions ke sunt botez devant le rey, de queus le plus porroient estre espleytez par chanceler e par justices, purveu est ke tutes les peticions ke tuchent le sel veynent primes al chanceler, e ceus ke tuchent le escheker veynent al escheker, e ceus ke tuchent justices u ley de terre veinent a justices, e ceus ke tuchent juerie veynent a justices de la juerie. Et si les bosoigns seent si grantz u si de grace ke le chanceler e ces autres ne le pussent fere sanz le rey, dunk il les porterunt par lur meins demeine devant le rey pur saver ent sa volente, ensi qe nule peticion ne veigne devaunt le roy e son conseil fors par les mains des avauntditz chaunceller

---

² For assistance in the translation of law French and Latin passages here and elsewhere in the booklet the editor is indebted to Joseph R. Berrigan, Professor of Medieval History at the University of Georgia. [Editor's note.]

a les autres chef ministres, ensi ke le rey e sun consail pussent sanz charge de autre busoignes entendre a grosse busoignes de sun reaume et de ses foreines terres.

[Because the people who come to the royal parliament are often upset and disturbed, to great disadvantage both of themselves and of the court, by the multitude of petitions that come before the king, of which the greater part could be handled by the chancellors and the justices, it has been provided that all the petitions that have to do with the salt tax should go to the chancellor, those that have to do with the exchequer should go to the exchequer, those that have to do with justice or the law of the land should come before the justices, those that have to do with the Jews should go to the justices of the Jews. And if these needs are so great, or if the chancellor and the others cannot do it without the king, then let them carry it in their hands in the morning before the king to hear his will in the matter, in such a way that no petition shall come before the king and his council except from the hands of the aforementioned chancellor and the other chief ministers, in order that the king and his council, without attention to other matters, pay heed to the great needs of the realm and of his foreign lands.]

The object of these arrangements is evidently to reduce to a minimum the number of petitions actually brought before the king and his council in parliament. As many as possible are to be disposed of by the chancellor, by the officers of the exchequer, by the judges, by the justices of the Jews. Only those petitions concerning business which is "so great or so much a matter of grace" that it cannot be settled without the king — only such petitions are to be brought in parliament before the king and his council; and the memorandum expressly explains that all this is in order that the king and his council may, without being troubled with "other business," be able to attend to "the great

business of his kingdom and of his foreign lands."

This very significant document shows indeed that petitions in parliament were apt to be multitudinous, and that the answering of them was undoubtedly one of the functions normally performed in parliament: but the whole emphasis of the document is upon those things which have to come in parliament before the king and his council, the things described in the memorandum as "the great business of his kingdom and of his foreign lands": the whole object of the memorandum is to try to ensure that petitions do not stand in the way of that "great business." Now some "great business" would doubtless arise out of the petitions that were "so great or so much a matter of grace" that they could not be answered without consulting the king, but most of "the great business of his kingdom and of his foreign lands" would arise simply because it was propounded in parliament by, or on behalf of, the king himself. We know that he often announced in the writs of summons what some of this "great business" would be, as for instance in the writs for the parliament of February 1305, which stated that the subject of the "stabilimentum terre nostre Scocie" would be coming up for consideration. A little later, when the proceedings of parliaments begin to be recorded in rather more detail, we find that they usually opened with a speech by one of the king's ministers setting out the "causes of summons." We may be very sure, too, that if in any parliament the king and his council desired that legislation be promulgated or taxes granted, such legislation or taxation would rank as "great business." Quite clearly, the royal officials who drew up the memorandum of 1280 were proceeding on the assumption that "great business" as well as multitudinous petitions must be expected, and expected as a matter of course, in any parliament. In other words, they considered that the transacting of "great business" — which would include such things as taxation and legislation when they arose — was as normal a feature of parliaments as was the dispensing of "justice"; that even if such things as taxation or legislation did not happen to come up in any given parliament, nevertheless "great business" would come up in some form or other; and that if there was any question of priority, the priority pertained, not to petitions, but to "great business."

It being thus evident that "justice" and "great business" — *both of them* — were regarded by authoritative opinion in the thirteenth century as *equally* normal concerns of parliament, is it nevertheless justifiable still to maintain the twentieth-century doctrine that the dispensing of "justice" was an "essential" function, while the transacting of "great business" was "non-essential"? Such a position could be successfully defended only if either or both of two suppositions could be established. The first of these suppositions would be, that in the Middle Ages parliaments provided the only occasions on which the English king could be petitioned for "justice." The second of the two suppositions would be, that in the Middle Ages it was only in parliaments that petitioners could expect their petitions to be answered *as of right*. Clearly, if parliaments really were the only occasions on which the king could be petitioned for "justice," and still more if they were the only occasions on which petitioners had *a legal right* to have an answer to their petitions, then the "judicial" functions performed in connection with petitions might be regarded as having at least some specific distinctiveness among the various functions that were performed in parliament. The first supposition, however, is ruled out by the evidence. The second has indeed been propounded as an hypothesis in an attempt to explain the difference between parliaments and cognate assemblies known as "great councils":

but the scholars who have so propounded it have not been able to verify it by evidence, and it must now be regarded as a waning rather than a working hypothesis.

If then we reject the latter-day doctrine that the dispensing of "justice" was the "essence" of parliament, and that the other functions — summarized in 1280 as "attending to the great business of the realm" — were merely something "added," and were therefore something "non-essential" which may and should be "stripped away": must we therefore proceed now to reverse the doctrine, and say that "attending to the great business of the realm" was the "essence" of parliament, and that the dispensing of "justice" was the "non-essential" function which was "added" and which may therefore be "stripped away"? The answer is that neither function may rightly be "stripped away" — that is, if we wish to see the pre-representative parliament as it really was. The evidence as a whole indicates that the functional "essence" of the pre-representative parliaments, so far from being "judicial," consisted rather in *not being* "judicial." Important "judicial" functions could be, and often were, performed in parliament, but the essence of its functions was not specifically judicial, any more than it was specifically legislative, or specifically taxative, or specifically anything. The essence of its function consisted in being *unspecific,* in being *omni*-competent, in ranging over the whole field of lay government, in exercising (always, of course, in association with the king, who was "its head, its beginning and its end") those functions of government which, in the earliest extant description of English parliaments, are summarised as "viewing the state of the realm and treating the common business of the kingdom and of the king."

# Can One Really Discover the Nature of Early Parliaments?

## SIR MAURICE POWICKE

Sir Maurice Powicke (1879–1963) studied with T. F. Tout at Manchester and later became Regius Professor of Modern History at Oxford. From 1933–1939 he served as president of the Royal Historical Society. Powicke approached medieval institutions from the viewpoint of the men who made them, reminding readers in *King Henry III and the Lord Edward* (1947) that "history, even constitutional history, is the history of persons." Other publications of Powicke include the *Loss of Normandy* (1913), *Stephen Langton* (The Ford Lectures, 1928), *The Thirteenth Century, 1216–1307* (Oxford History of England, 1953), and several works on medieval life and thought. In the selection below, taken from *King Henry III and the Lord Edward*, Powicke cautions against "too eager definition" of early English parliaments.

THE WORD "PARLIAMENT" has been used in the previous pages. A case of the royal right to big fish washed up on the sea-shore was adjourned from the exchequer into a parliament. Henry of Bath's trial is said to have taken place in the exciting atmosphere of a parliament. The holders of liberties by charter were invited to bring their troubles to the exchequer at a time when a great council was most likely to assemble for the feast of St. Edward. A problem raised by a royal writ was to be discussed by the council at the feast of St. Edward. And if we look around, we find that the word "parliament" is becoming a very common word, and we find also a tendency to concentrate important or exceptional judicial business at times early in the exchequer half-year, after Michaelmas and Easter, and early in the other terms observed by the courts, for example at Candlemas, a fortnight or so after the beginning of Hilary term. Occasionally, once as early as 1242, and several times early in 1248, the word "parliament" is used when business is adjourned in this way. As the years pass, the relation between times of

parliament and the times to which public or judicial business is referred becomes closer. The two movements, if indeed they were two and not in fact one movement, appear to come together. And yet, at the same time, we read throughout this period of great councils or parliaments which met to discuss the royal need and to ventilate baronial grievances, with no obvious relation to normal public business, and when the king's courts were not in regular session. The king and his council seem to stretch the capacity of the royal household to comprise parliament, yet parliament does not quite fit into the routine of the court. Our safest line of approach is by way of the crown.

At certain times in the year much business had to be done. Council, judges, barons of the exchequer had to work together as a group. In the course of a period of this kind, during Henry's absence in France, in the second part of October 1254, the regent, Richard of Cornwall, left Westminster for Windsor. The election of a new mayor of London was made at a time which in Henry's reign came just before

From Sir Maurice Powicke, *King Henry III and the Lord Edward*, 2 volumes (London, 1947), I, pp. 338–342. Reprinted by permission of The Clarendon Press.

the end of the regnal year at the end of October. In this year the new mayor could not be presented at the exchequer, as he should have been, on the morrow of his election, "because the barons of the exchequer were then in parliament at Windsor." The chronicler describes this congested period as a time of parliament, though the great parliaments known to history might be held at other times. On the other hand, certain kinds of business required the attention and consent of the great council as a whole. King and barons did not altogether agree on this matter. The barons, for example, thought that new judicial writs, authorizing new kinds of process, required their consent, whereas the king considered the authorization of council and judges to be sufficient; but there was no disagreement about the principle that some business was best done when the magnates had been gathered together. In 1243, before the newly elected Archbishop Boniface had entered upon his duties, the prior and monks of Canterbury fell foul of the English bishops. They were accused to the king of stretching out their hands to the "liberties of the churches." They interfered in matters which pertained to the dignity of the archbishopric. King Henry was in Bordeaux when the complaints of the bishops were brought to his notice. He wrote to them, to the prior and convent, and to the guardians of the realm. All proceedings must be stayed until his return. Without his council and other magnates he would make no ordinance on an issue which tended "to change the state of the realm." He would convoke a council of the whole realm at which "we may more freely consider how to bring you back to agreement in this difficult business." One of the first cases in which a parliament, so called, was concerned in a judicial action occurred in 1248. The judges of the Bench at Westminster had awarded damages to the abbot and convent of Tintern against the archdeacon of Lincoln. Some question arose, and further action against the archdeacon

was stayed until the parliament to be held a fortnight after Candlemas (i.e. on 15 February 1248), "because the king wishes to have a discussion about the proceedings." In the same parliament a sentence of outlawry was reversed because it had not followed the procedure required by the law and custom of the realm. "It was decided in our court before us and our whole parliament that the outlawry aforesaid was to be considered null and void." This was a famous parliament, one of those in which the magnates had traversed the conduct of affairs and Henry's method of government. It was the parliament, also, at which "the magnates of our realm were in no wise willing to agree that the fruits of vacant churches in the gift of laymen should be given for one year in aid of the church of Canterbury, as granted by the apostolic see." Henry had acquiesced in this decision. "We forbid you," he wrote to the bishop of Norwich, "to take any such action in your diocese, until we have had further talk with the aforesaid magnates. Without them we wish to do nothing in the matter." The precious writs which tell us these things supplement the narrative of Matthew Paris. They are not concerned with the disputes between king and magnates. They reveal a kind of intimacy between them in parliament. They fall into line with the tendency to arrange the conduct of business so that the increasing pressure upon the exchequer, the judges, the council, should be relieved by a more emphatic terminal rhythm.

The mystery which attends on the beginnings of parliament is not peculiar to these particular happenings. It is the mystery which attends on all beginnings, when men are doing things because they are convenient and do not attach conscious significance to them, still less consider what the distant outcome of their acts may be. The word was in the air, the materials were to hand. To track down every nerve in the body politic and locate each impulse, as though they carried some secret message, is as futile as to read into the rivulets which compose the upmost waters of the Thames a foresight of the wharves and shipping in its spacious estuary. Nor should we injure the fragile uncertainties of these beginnings by too eager definition. Some would deny any relevance to the great dispute about parliament in the tendencies at work in the court of King Henry. Others would press too hard the coincidence of interest between the meetings of the great council and the arrangement of judicial business in the law terms. It is safer to state the facts. "Parliament" was not what lawyers call a term of art. It might merely mean a colloquy or it might describe a meeting of magnates summoned to a stated place at a stated time for a particular purpose. In neither case did it suggest specialized functions. A baron in the Welsh marches whose bailiff gathered the vassals together for business had his parliament; and when Marchers and Welshmen met in conference they had a parliament. Similarly, the tradition of great annual feasts attended by the king's vassals had never been lost, but their regularity had been broken, whereas the great councils summoned to treat with the king on the affairs of the realm had too often assumed the character of parlays between divided interests. In Henry's reign under new conditions the Norman tradition tended to revive, yet at the same time the great councils tended to express an independence of their own. This does not mean that there were two kinds of parliament, but that there was a distinction between the conditions which made the king and his servants on the one hand and the magnates on the other aware of the value of parliament. In Edward I's time the coincidence in time and place between parliaments regarded from these two points of view is complete. Parliaments, except possibly, though not certainly, during Edward's absence in Gascony (1286–9), were held nearly every year, once, twice, or thrice, generally in Westminster and notably at Michaelmas and Easter. The presence of knights and burgesses was not yet a criterion of parliament; it became a general rule only during the first quarter of the fourteenth century. A parliament, we are told, implied the judicial activity which arose, as we have seen, from the co-operation of king and administration in the affairs of state. If this activity were not exercised in an assembly, even though knights and burgesses were present, the assembly was not, we are told, described in official documents as a parliament. Yet developments in England were due to the appreciation of the twofold nature of parliament, whereas in France, where the stress lay on its judicial nature, the history of parliament took a different course.

King and magnates were more closely allied than they knew. Their quarrels were domestic, inside the great house of the king. Their relations had been defined in the great councils of 1234, and when the charters were confirmed in 1237. Their troubles were largely due to bad temper. On both sides, nay, on all sides intelligence and good sense were marred by lack of restraint.

In 1255 the marshal, Roger Bigod, earl of Norfolk, whose wife was a daughter of William the Lion, interceded with Henry for Robert de Ros, the lord of Wark in Northumberland. Robert had incurred Henry's displeasure by his tactless tutorship of the young king of Scotland and the young queen, Henry's daughter. Henry, as usual, flew into a rage and called the earl a traitor. "You lie," said the earl, "I have never been a traitor nor shall I ever be. If you are just, how can you harm me?" The King retorted: "I can seize your corn and thrash it and sell it." "Do so," said the earl, "and I will send back your threshers without their heads." Friends interposed to separate the pair; but, adds Matthew Paris, the windy words bred anger and hatred.

History, even constitutional history, is the history of persons. We are dealing with men who lived well, loved tournaments, and liked romances better than law books. And Henry had the tongue of an asp.

# II. THE ARRIVAL OF REPRESENTATIVES: WHY WERE THEY SUMMONED AND WHAT DID THEY DO?

## The Representatives as Tools of an Aspiring Autocrat

### DÉSIRÉ PASQUET

Désiré Pasquet (1870–1928), a native of France, concentrated his research and teaching career upon the history of the English-speaking peoples, publishing *Londres et les ouvriers de Londres* (1914), *Essai sur les origines de la Chambre des Communes* (1914), and the *Histoire des Etats-Unis* (1924). He studied in America in 1925 under a grant from the Rockefeller Foundation and returned to l'Ecole des Hautes Etudes, Paris, in 1926 as director of studies in United States history. In the *Essay on the Origins of the House of Commons*, from which the selection below is taken, Pasquet emphasizes the petitioning role of knights and burgesses in parliament, suggesting that Edward I summoned representatives of these groups so that he might break the feudal structure and aspire to absolute rule.

WHAT MOTIVES induced Edward I thus to compel representatives of the lesser gentry and the freemen of the counties and towns, as well as the prelates and barons, to do suit of court? Did he really perceive, as Stubbs suggests, that "a strong king must be the king of a united people" and that a people, "to be united, must possess a balanced constitution, in which no class possesses absolute and independent power, none is powerful enough to oppress without remedy?" Was he chiefly concerned to obtain the consent of his subjects to the increasing taxes which he imposed on them? Such has been, since the seventeenth century, the view of a large number of historians. Or did he merely wish to reform administration, to be informed about his sheriffs, to receive petitions addressed to the crown, and to provide for the collection of aids? This theory, which very much reduces the importance of the earliest representatives of the commons, has been put forward by Riess and supported with arguments that are not without force.

Historians have often quoted and highly praised that passage in the writ of 1295, addressed to the prelates, in which Edward I says:

As a most just law, established by the careful providence of the holy princes, orders and decrees that what affects all should be approved by all, even so very evidently should common dangers be met with means provided in common.

From D. Pasquet, *Essay on the Origins of the House of Commons*, trans., R. G. D. Laffan (Cambridge, 1925), Shoe String Press edn., Hamden Conn., 1964), pp. 171–174, 176–177, 197–202, 204–210, 213–216, 225–226. Reprinted by permission of Cambridge University Press.

Edward then dwells on the dishonest seizure of Gascony by the king of France and concludes with an order to the bishops to attend parliament accompanied by their clergy.

The phrase *"quod omnes tangit ab omnibus approbetur"* is, according to Stubbs, a summary of Edward's policy. The gathering of deputies from counties and towns to the parliament of 1295 was but an application of this principle. Deliberately for twenty years Edward prepared for this innovation. He perceived that the English people desired to take its place in the constitution of the country; and, when the appropriate moment seemed to him to have come, he called the whole nation to participate in the government of the realm. Two years later, it is true, he seems to have wished to retrace his steps. A violent conflict broke out between him and his subjects over his proposed expedition to Flanders. Edward confiscated the wool, seized ecclesiastical property and tried to levy aids to which parliament had not agreed. But that was because at the moment he was at war with Scotland and France and was also at odds with Boniface VIII. In these exceptional circumstances he tried to assume dictatorship and "failing, he yielded gracefully."

If Edward I really entertained the designs attributed to him, he should not be compared, as he is by Stubbs, to Alfonso the Wise, to Philippe le Bel, or to Saint Louis, but to one of those great men of rare political genius, who have at intervals appeared in human history, to Julius Caesar or to Augustus. But such designs are so utterly opposed to the conceptions of Edward's time and to his own authoritarian temperament as not even to have an air of probability. In 1305 Edward obtained the pope's cancellation of the Great Charter and his own release from all his promises to his people. How can we believe that, in calling the representatives of the counties and towns to his parliament, he desired of his own free will to share his power with the nation? We may further observe that the phrase, which is held to summarize Edward's whole policy, does not appear in the writ ordering the sheriffs to proceed to elections, but only in that addressed to the prelates. If, therefore, we wish to give it any precise significance, it can only be applied to the representatives of the inferior clergy. But in reality the phrase seems to have been a commonplace of thirteenth-century political literature, borrowed, as Stubbs himself points out, from Justinian's Code. It is but a part of that store of philosophical maxims and flowers of rhetoric, on which English chancery clerks loved to draw, especially when addressing the clergy, who seemed to them more capable than the laity of appreciating elegance of style. Edward was so little disposed to see that what concerned all should be approved by all, that after 1295, as before that date, he often reserved the most important questions for the consideration of his barons or merely of his council, without calling representatives of the commons to a parliament.

It is clear that Edward's object, in assembling deputies of the counties and towns, was not to make them participate in his legislative activities. Legislation was a royal prerogative, in which subjects took no part, except to give counsel, when the king demanded it of them. . . .

Neither did Edward I summon the delegates of the commons in order to consult with them on questions of general policy. . . .

The desire for financial support, on the contrary, has been considered by most historians to have been the principal cause for the convocation of deputies of the commons. . . . The right of voting the budget has become so much the most important prerogative of modern parliaments that we are naturally inclined to suppose that financial questions played the chief part in their origins. On certain occasions, indeed, as for example in 1294 and 1306, the representatives of the commons seem to have been summoned for the sole purpose of being asked for an extraordinary grant. But we know that these representatives were summoned by Edward to numerous parliaments (1283, 1298, 1300, 1302, 1305, 1307), at which no demand of a financial kind seems to have been made by the king.

The documents published in the collection of *Rotuli Parliamentorum* and, for the parliament of 1305, in the *Memoranda* of Maitland show us that in these parliaments, as in nearly all the parliaments of Edward I, most of the work consisted of hearing the suits which the king had reserved for himself in parliament and examining the petitions presented to the king and his council. Important questions of policy and legislation might be dealt with in conferences between the king and the *fideles* [trusted friends] whom he summoned, but suits and petitions were the normal business of parliamentary routine. Thus parliament, in its essential functions, appears as the continuation of the old *curia regis* [king's council], as the high court of justice of the realm, capable of redressing wrongs which could not be redressed by the common law.

The part which the knights and burgesses could take in the hearing of *placita* was evidently very small. The documents do not mention their presence. In 1305 suits were determined after their departure. Indeed, as we have already said, the house of commons has never claimed a share in the judicial functions of the house of lords. If knights or burgesses were summoned before the king in a judicial matter, they came as individuals, to provide information, or as pleaders, to further the interests of a town or county. Thus at the parliament of 1305 amongst the four citizens, to whom Salisbury entrusted the conduct of its litigation against its bishop in the king's court, were the two deputies of that city.

For our purpose the petitions are of much greater importance than the *placita*; an importance that has not wholly escaped the notice of Riess, who devotes a few lines of his monograph to it, but does not adequately dwell on this point, which to us seems essential.

The practice of approaching the king and his council to complain of an injustice or to demand a favour dates back to a period long before the reign of Edward I. But it seems that in earlier times the petitioner appeared in person before the council and explained the nature of his demand orally. By the end of the thirteenth century this form of procedure was rendered impossible by the great number of petitions and the enlarged activity of the royal administration. Attendance in person and oral demand were supplanted by written petition. It was even found necessary to systematize the filing and examination of these petitions, many of which were of very little importance and only wasted the time of the king and his councillors. In the eighth (1279–1280) and the twenty-first (1292–1293) years of Edward I measures were taken to classify the petitions and to reserve for the king's personal attention only those matters which were so important that they could not otherwise be dealt with.

In 1305 the king, being then absent from London, gave instructions in advance to the chancellor, commanded a public proclamation to be made in the great hall of Westminster, in West Cheap and at the Guild-hall, requiring all with petitions to submit to present them before the first Sunday in Lent (7th March), and ordered that as many petitions as possible should be examined before his return.

The number of petitions presented at this parliament, on which we have exceptionally complete information, was about 450. They were received and classified by a commission of four persons: a judge, a high official of the exchequer, and two clerks of the chancery. When parliament met, a special commission was appointed to examine the petitions concerning Scotland, another those of Gascony, a third those of Ireland and the Channel Islands.

Similar commissions were probably nominated for the English petitions. The king himself went vigorously to work. On Sunday, the 7th March, thirty-two petitions were examined before him.

The status of the petitioners and the nature and importance of the petitions varied considerably. Most of the petitions (over 400) were presented by individuals, and most of these, as Maitland points out, could not have been debated in an assembly. For example, the prior of Bridlington complains that Thomas de Monceaux will not allow him, or his people, or the people of the district, to cross his land, as has always been their custom, to go to the king's market at Kingston-upon-Hull. The university of Cambridge begs the king to found a college. Thomas de Moriley asks the king to restore to him his father's fiefs in Cumberland; which fiefs had been confiscated because his father had been hostile to the king in the Scottish war; but the petitioner had ever been loyal to the king. Robert Treyfot, imprisoned for having allowed a prisoner, whom he had been ordered to deliver to the sheriff of Essex, to escape, implores the king to pardon him. Alice, the divorced wife of John de Beaumont, protests that her late husband has returned, ravaged her domains and seized her charters and jewels. In many cases the council or the commissioners appointed to examine the petition confine themselves to informing the petitioner as to his line of procedure — he should obtain a writ from chancery, he should appear before the exchequer, he should await the results of an inquest, etc.

But some of these petitions are of more general interest. Simon le Parker complains that the jury, ordered to pronounce on the facts on account of which he is in prison, has been challenged out of pure malice, and consequently he is still in the prison of Canterbury. The king and council reply with a ruling, which is later considered to be an ordinance and as such appears in the *Statutes of the Realm*. Possibly the ordinance of trailbaston,[1] which was also made at this parliament, originated similarly in a private petition.

None of those sent to the parliament of February 1305 as representatives of a county or a town figure among the members of the commissions which were nominated to examine petitions and whose composition is known to us. Some may have been included in the commissions for English petitions; but it is unlikely. The council may sometimes have consulted knights and burgesses on the petitions that concerned their county or town. It would have been a convenient method of verifying the statements of the petitioners. But it was above all as being themselves petitioners that the knights and burgesses came to parliament and appeared before the council.

The parliament rolls of 1305 contain eight petitions presented by counties (including one from the community of the bishopric of Durham, which had no representative in parliament) and 23 presented by twelve towns (all, it appears, represented in parliament). Like the petitions of individuals, amongst which they are enrolled, these petitions from communities deal with the most varied topics. They contain many pecuniary claims, which are usually referred to the exchequer. The people of Cumberland demand payment for the provisions taken by the sheriff for the king's larder. They also complain that the collectors of the fifteenth have restored nothing on account of the amounts which the king ordered to be repaid. Carlisle also claims the value of the barley and oats "borrowed" by the king for his army in Scotland. Dunwich asks for assistance towards the repair of her harbour, which has been wrecked by a storm, and that against her dues to the

---

[1] Ordinances of trailbaston were issued by Edward I and subsequent kings against those who "carry a club." Growing incidences of robbery and assault, resulting from the king's long absences on foreign wars, made the special ordinances necessary. [Editor's note.]

king shall be set a credit for the enormous losses in ships and men, which she has sustained in the king's wars. The people of York complain that the exchequer is demanding the price of a quantity of wine, which they had bought from the king's cellarer in the time of Henry III and for which they had paid.

Numerous petitions refer to the privileges of counties and towns and request their confirmation or extension. The community of the bishopric of Durham claim a charter which has remained in chancery. Carlisle demands the return of her liberties, which had been suspended after the burning of the city's charters. Cockermouth asks permission to establish a right of pontage[2] for the repair of her bridge. Worcester asks permission to establish a right of murage.[3] Norwich wishes her right of murage prolonged for seven years (the king only prolonged it for five). Several towns (Appleby, Dunwich) complain of illicit markets established in their neighbourhood. . . .

Amongst the other petitions presented by communities to this parliament of February 1305, we may quote that of Northumberland, which asks that judges *de banco* should visit the county, hold assizes and take inquests; that of Lancashire, requesting the nomination of a commission of two persons to hold an inquest on the malefactors who trouble the king's peace; those of Cumberland which refer to the deforestations effected since 1301 and have a more general interest. . . .

The parliament of 1305 affords us other examples of collective petitions besides those from towns and counties. There is a petition in which "the poor men of the land of England" demand measures against those who are entrusted with the making of inquests or form part of assizes and juries and allow themselves to be corrupted by litigants; and another against

the ordinaries of dioceses who are usurping the functions of the king's judges. These are probably petitions from all the representatives of the commons, knights and burgesses together. Two other petitions were presented in the name of the earls, barons and community of the realm. Their object was to prevent religious houses, both of men and women, from sending money abroad to the superiors of the motherhouses of their orders. To these petitions which he may have himself suggested, the king replies that in full parliament, "with the consent of the prelates, earls, barons and others of the realm," he has provided for the matter in a statute "in the following form." But on the roll the space that follows remains blank. The statute *De asportatis religiosorum* was only promulgated two years later at the parliament of Carlisle.

During the three weeks which they passed at this parliament of 1305 one of the chief functions of the knights and burgesses was certainly the presentation of the petitions of their county or town and the defence of these petitions before the council. We saw above that they took their leave before the discussion on Scottish affairs began. The only question of general importance on which the king seems to have consulted them was that of the tallage paid by English religious to foreign houses. Later on the Articles of 1309 also show us that in the presentation of petitions the representatives of the commons saw one of the essential reasons for their presence in parliament. They complain that "the knights and the men of the cities, boroughs and other towns," who come to parliament at the king's order, on behalf of themselves and the people, "and have petitions to submit on account of wrongs and oppressions done to them that cannot be redressed by the common law or in any other way except by special warrant," find none to receive their petitions; which is contrary to the custom of parliament under Edward I. The king decided to meet their wishes. At the parliament of Lincoln in

[2] Pontage was a right to levy a tax for the maintenance and repair of bridges. [Editor's note.]
[3] Murage was a right to levy a tax for the building or repairing of town walls. [Editor's note.]

1316 the organization of parliamentary business was almost the same as in 1305. Gradually collective petitions presented by the whole body of the representatives of the commons assumed greater importance and wider application till they became in fact bills, which only needed the royal approbation to become statutes. In this way, during the fourteenth century, the character of parliament continued to change. The presentation and examination of private petitions passed more and more into the background, and that function of parliament was inherited by the council. Meanwhile parliament itself, by means of collective petitions, developed from a court of justice into a legislative assembly.

There is no doubt that Edward I did not foresee such a development of the system of petitions; and that he did not summon knights and burgesses to parliament in order to allow them to submit fully prepared legislative proposals in the form of petitions. To redress wrongs and oppressions done to his subjects certainly appeared to him one of the first duties of the king; but the prerogatives of the king could not fail to gain by these periodic "great days," at which all his subjects brought their complaints before him. The petitions of the communities, counties and towns, gave him exact information on the state of the kingdom. They enabled him to supervise the smallest details of the behaviour of his officials, to repress encroachments by great lords or abuses of their authority by the clergy. . . .

This brings us to an idea which was, we believe, one of the bases of Edward's policy. The convocation of deputies of the commons was the outcome not only of practical needs and administrative requirements, but also of a new conception of the relations that should exist between the king and his subjects. If we did not hesitate to use terms which are anachronistic, we would be tempted to say that, throughout his reign, Edward's object was to transform his vassals and sub-vassals into subjects and feudal aids into taxes; and that the convocation of deputies of the commons was one of the most effective means which he employed to carry out that transformation.

Edward had the most exalted idea of his own authority. He claimed to be not only the suzerain of his vassals, but the king of all his subjects. Although he availed himself to the utmost of every legal advantage given him by feudal custom, he did not respect one of the fundamental principles of that custom, namely the distinction between immediate vassals and sub-vassals. That distinction he set aside whenever he thought it necessary to do so. Indeed he set himself systematically to destroy it.

His reign opened with the great inquest whose results were entered in the *Rotuli Hundredorum*. [Hundred Rolls]. The object of the inquest was that the king might be exactly informed on the extent of the rights of the crown and the nature of the encroachments which those rights had suffered. The commissioners were to obtain information on the lands which were then in the king's possession and on those which had once been in his possession and were so no longer. . . .

Despite their protests the holders of liberties had to produce their title-deeds. Inquests *Quo warranto*, regulated by the Statute of Gloucester (1278), were carried on without interruption during a large part of the reign. The royal judges at first displayed an exaggerated severity, picking holes in the terms of charters granted by previous kings and refusing to take account of prescription. It is true that they were obliged to diminish their pretentions; but, even if they failed to recover for the crown the lands and rights that had been formally ceded, their efforts at least succeeded in preventing the formation of new liberties and in checking the movement which threatened to withdraw a considerable portion of the land from the direct authority of the king. On one essential point the king successfully imposed his will; in 1290 the statute *Quia emptores* put an end to subinfeudation.

Subinfeudation was highly objectionable

from the point of view of royal authority. When fiefs were so multiplied that, in some cases, each one was no more than a twentieth or a fortieth of a knight's fee, the services, which his tenants-in-chief owed the king, were not forthcoming. . . . The feudal host became inadequate for a serious campaign and the king was obliged to have recourse to mercenaries paid by himself; while the old feudal taxation, when levied, only produced an insignificant amount. For these reasons the king in 1290 promulgated the statute *Quia emptores,* by the terms of which the purchaser of land became the vassal not of the vendor, but of the vendor's overlord. The magnates, who composed the parliament, accepted the measure because it appeared to them to serve their interests as well as those of the king, and perhaps also because the king granted them certain concessions. . . .

The king went much further in his efforts to extirpate mesne lords and to bring all his subjects under his immediate authority. It was in pursuance of this policy that he took steps on several occasions to force those of his subjects — as well sub-vassals as tenants-in-chief — who had revenue of a certain amount, to become knights and serve in the host when he summoned them. Similar orders had several times been issued in the reign of Henry III, but appear to have been applied only to tenants-in-chief. Under Edward I this distinction disappeared. . . .

These experiments, which were not always crowned with success, are to be in part explained by the king's financial needs. The imposition of the duties of knighthood on as many of his subjects as possible was a means of obtaining a larger revenue from fines. But we believe that it would be wrong to reduce a policy pursued by Edward I with so much perseverance to mere financial sharp practice. With regard to military service the king proposed to abolish the existing distinction between tenants-in-chief and sub-vassals. By summoning representatives of the knights and burgesses to his parliament, he abolished that distinction with regard to suit of court. In the one case as in the other he was destroying the feudal framework of society. . . .

The formation of the house of commons has long been represented as the last step in a development which began with the Great Charter, was continued by the Provisions of Oxford and the great parliament of 1265, and ended in the "model" parliament of 1295. This development was held to have been caused by the alliance of the magnates, gentry and bourgeoisie, who all united to oppose the excessive power of the crown and succeeded in limiting the royal authority. But the study of the documents has led us to quite other conclusions. The nation did not demand representation in the king's parliament. It was the king who imposed on his subjects the duty of sending him their representatives.

Edward I changed an occasional expedient into a regular custom, not in order to associate the whole nation with himself in the work of government, but in order to strengthen the royal power. He only summoned the representatives of the commons when such a course seemed to him to serve his own interests; and often the most important agenda were discussed in their absence. If in the end he made a practice of summoning them almost regularly, this was because he perceived that the previous consent of the knights and burgesses greatly facilitated the collection of aids and even enabled the government to collect rather more than would otherwise have been possible. Another reason was that the petitions, in which the delegates of the communities begged him to redress wrongs irremediable by the ordinary processes of the law, gave him full information on the condition of his kingdom and enabled him to make all aware of the strength of the royal arm. Every abuse of power by a great lord, every injustice by a servant of the crown, every invasion of the royal rights was denounced before the king's court; and thus the sessions of the full parliaments carried on the grand inquest of the beginning of the reign. Lastly, the assemblies of representatives from counties and towns embodied one of the fundamental ideas of Edward's policy. In parliament, as formed by him, the old feudal distinction between tenants-in-chief and sub-vassals was entirely abolished. The king had before him only subjects. Despite its feudal form, the summoning of the commons was an essentially anti-feudal measure, the object of which was to strengthen the central power and to sub-

ject all the inhabitants of the realm, of whatever rank in the feudal hierarchy, to the direct authority of the monarch. In this respect Edward continued the policy of Henry II and emulated Philippe le Bel.

But Edward's plans did not succeed; or rather they succeeded only in part. The assembly of representatives from counties and towns did indeed rapidly achieve the destruction of the feudal system of society. But it did not result in an increase of the royal power, as Edward had hoped.

# Representation as a Propaganda Technique

## HELEN MAUD CAM

Throughout a long career as teacher and scholar in England and America, Helen Cam (1885—  ) has fixed her attention upon the local community and its institutions in the Middle Ages. Her most significant work, *The Hundred and the Hundred Rolls* appeared in 1930; it has been followed by numerous articles and addresses on related subjects, many of which were reprinted in *Liberties and Communities in Medieval England* (1944) and *Law-finders and Law-makers in Medieval England* (1963). She has worked actively with the *International Commission for the History of Representative and Parliamentary Institutions* since its beginning in 1937, serving as president of that body in 1949. The *Commission* honored Helen Cam in 1960 by dedicating to her volumes XXIII and XXIV of the *Studies . . .* [on] *the History of Representative and Parliamentary Institutions*. In the selection below, taken from volume III (1939) of those same *Studies*, she suggests that Edward I may have called representatives to parliament in order to secure at the local level a favorable reception of his programs.

I N SPITE OF ALL that has been written about the early history of representative institutions in England, we still know very little about the actual relations between the representatives and the communities whom they represented, or, to use modern language, between the members of parliament and their constituencies. We know more about the theory of representation than about its practice, and our approach to the theory is more often from the side of the central government than from that of the locality, more often from the historical than from the contemporary standpoint.

There are four aspects of this relationship on which some work has been done of recent years, though there is still a wide field for inquiry. The first is of pivotal constitutional importance, and has long

From H. M. Cam, "The Relation of English Members of Parliament to Their Constituencies in the Fourteenth Century: a Neglected Text," *Studies Presented to the International Commission for the History of Representative and Parliamentary Institutions,* III (Louvain, 1939), pp. 143–147. Reprinted by permission of the author and of the publisher.

been the subject of study; it is the power of the members to bind the communities that elected them. On the association of representation with consent to taxation depends the sovereignty of the British parliament. The latest contribution to this question as it bears on the relation of the member to his constituency is Mr. J. G. Edwards' essay which appeared in 1932 on the formula *cum plena potestate* in the parliamentary writs of summons. He pointed out that Pasquet was not justified in saying that contemporary chronicles made no reference to the practice of representation; the chronicler Bartholomew Cotton in 1294 had observed "vocati sunt milites de quolibet comitatu qui haberent potestatem obligandi comitatum" [knights were summoned from a particular county who would have power to bind the county]; and by a comparison of the formulae used he showed how the principle was defined and established that the knights had power to bind their shires to the payment of the taxes to which they had assented. It is possible that this relationship between electors and elected was expressed in commissions, sealed with the borough seal, which the burgesses brought with them to parliament, giving them full powers to act, though even so we find the burgesses of King's Lynn referring to their constituents during a session and asking for further instructions.

In the second place it has been suggested that the electing body entrusted to their representatives petitions to be delivered to the king in parliament. Dr. Ludwig Riess considered this the main purpose for which representation was introduced by the English kings, and Dr. Pasquet accepts his view that the most important function of the members was to report to the central government the grievances of the localities, especially against the officials of the crown. This function, however, has been assumed rather than proved. It is quite certain that petitions could be and were presented to the king at "parliaments" to which no representatives had been summoned. On the other hand, when representatives did attend, we cannot prove that, to begin with, they regarded the presentation of petitions as part of their duty. Mr. George Haskins has recently investigated, for the last seventeen years of the reign of Edward I, the question of how far the representatives who attended parliaments actually presented petitions. In this period 11 parliaments were attended by representatives, and 63 petitions from constituencies are still in existence. Of the 37 shires represented, 15 sent in petitions; of the 165 boroughs, 40 sent in petitions. But there is absolutely no evidence that these petitions were presented by the elected representatives of the shires and boroughs. Twelve petitions were indeed presented by members of parliament, but these concerned their own private interests and not the affairs of the community they represented. It seems quite possible that they did deliver petitions from their communities, and also from individuals living in those communities, but it has not been proved. The only references yet noticed of the choice of representatives to state the grievances of a community suggest that these were *ad hoc* delegates, not the members already elected by royal command. In 1290 the poor men of Norfolk petitioned *per procuratos juratores;* in 1299 four men were chosen by the mayor and aldermen of London "ad prosequendum negotia civitatis coram rege et consilio in parliamento" [to conduct the business of the city in the presence of the king and his council in parliament]. For the reign of Edward I, at least, investigation has failed to produce evidence that the members presented petitions in parliament from their communities. Constitutionally speaking, the common petition presented in parliament is so much more important than the petitions from the separate communities that it is not surprising that comparatively little attention has been paid to the question of the private petition brought up ready made from the constituency. In the fourteenth century however there is more evidence. Miss

McKisack has found accounts in the town records of Norwich, King's Lynn, Cambridge and London of the elected representatives being requested to promote petitions in parliament (assisted, it is true, by other burgesses), as well as carrying out various kinds of business on behalf of their boroughs. At the end of the fourteenth century it was certainly considered the duty of members to present the grievances of their constituencies in parliament. . . .

A third possible function of the members in relation to their constituencies that still awaits investigation is that of serving as publicity agents. There were, no doubt, other agencies for spreading the news. Two early reports of parliaments are known; one the famous letter written from Oxford in 1258 describing the proceedings of the baronial reformers there, ending: "Ferociter procedunt barones in agendis suis; utinam bonum finem sortiantur!" [The barons conduct themselves fiercely in their affairs; would that they might achieve a good end!] This was copied with other documents into the chronicle of Burton Abbey, but whether it was private or for general consumption one cannot say. The second report was found recently by Mr. Richardson and Mr. Sayles among the *Parliamentary and Council Proceedings* at the Public Record Office, and printed by them in the *English Historical Review* of last July [1938]. It describes the doings of the parliament held at Carlisle in March 1307. It is headed *Noueles de parlement*, and does not appear to derive from an official source. Its editors believe that it was a commercial production; a news letter, directed probably to an ecclesiastical public. Unlike the Oxford letter it does not appear to be supporting any faction or pushing any view: it is not a piece of propaganda. On the other hand, it would seem that the possibility of using the elected representatives as agents of propaganda was realized at an early date, both by the crown and by its opponents the magnates. In 1327, in

the first parliament held after the deposition of Edward II, the commons, after taking an oath to uphold the new regime, asked for written records of what had been done in the parliament, and granted by the king and council, to carry back to their shires for proclamation by the sheriffs. In like manner, the deposition of Richard II was supported by the widespread circulation of the tendencious narrative enrolled on the roll of Henry IV's first parliament — a well known example of particularly successful propaganda. But the use of representatives as publicity agents originated, it would seem, with the crown. In 1261 Henry III commanded the presence of representatives of the shires "that they might see and understand for themselves that he was only aiming at the welfare of the whole community." In 1275 Edward I summoned knights to his first parliament, not to take an active part in drawing up the great Statute of Westminster I, but rather to hear and understand the reforms in local government which it contained, and to carry back to the community of the shire the explanation of the new provisions for restraining the corruptions and oppressions of their sheriffs. In 1283 and again in 1295 and 1307 Edward I was undoubtedly, like his contemporary Philippe le Bel, making use of the representative system for propaganda purposes; demonstrating to the communities of shire and borough, on whose material assistance he was bound to rely, the justice of his own cause against the villainy of his enemy, whether that enemy were David of Wales, Philip of France, or the Pope himself. The knights and burgesses were to carry back to their constituencies what they had learnt at the fountain head of these high matters of national policy.

As regards the thirteenth century we have no proof that the suggestion I have just made is valid: it is merely a plausible hypothesis. For the fourteenth century there is a little more evidence.

# The Representatives and Taxation

## CARL STEPHENSON

Carl Stephenson (1886–1954) taught at Cornell in the field of medieval economic history and the history of medieval institutions. In 1933 the Medieval Academy of America published his *Borough and Town: A Study of Urban Origins in England,* and in 1954 a collection of his articles appeared under the title *Medieval Institutions: Selected Essays.* With F. G. Marcham, Stephenson edited in 1937 the *Sources of English Constitutional History,* a book which contains a remarkably full collection of documents from Ethelbert to George VI. In the selection below, written in 1938, Stephenson offers a fiscal explanation for the origins of representation in England.

THIS PAPER, as will be seen, is based upon a series of distinctions, and to some it may appear significant that my plan was drafted between lectures on Gratian and Peter Lombard. Perhaps I *have* developed a scholastic bent; but I can at least affirm that my distinctions are drawn neither from theology nor from canon law. Rather, they have been suggested by an enforced reading of English constitutional sources during the past two years. The first distinction should be familiar to anyone who has studied the political oratory of Great Britain; the others to anyone who has followed the recent discussion of parliamentary origins. Reëmphasizing these distinctions will, I hope, serve to improve our understanding of representative institutions in medieval England.

A Conservative argument frequently heard in the halls of parliament has been that the house of commons holds discretionary power to act for the nation as a whole. A member, no matter how many people vote for him or what may be their local interests, should be regarded and should regard himself as a statesman rather than a mere delegate. The notion of a parliamentary mandate, a binding instruction laid upon either group or individual, is utterly foreign to the British constitution. Every loyal subject must fear and deplore the growing tendency to decide important issues by alleged appeals to the people — by exciting the voters to periodic states of frenzy and substituting a count of heads for political wisdom.

Such opinions — and they are by no means dead yet — rest upon a theory of representation dear to the hearts of the eighteenth-century Whigs. Writing to Sir Hercules Langrishe in 1792, Edmund Burke explained the matter as follows (the *distinctio prima* of this paper):

Virtual representation is that in which there is a community of interests, and a sympathy in feelings and desires, between those who act in the name of any description of people and the people in whose name they act, though the trustees are not actually chosen by them. This is virtual representation. Such a representation I think to be, in many cases, even better than the actual. It possesses most of its advantages and is free from many of its inconveniences; it corrects the irregularities in the literal representation, when the shifting current of human affairs, or the acting of public interest in different ways, carry it

From Carl Stephenson, "The Beginnings of Representative Government in England," *The Constitution Reconsidered,* ed. Conyers Read (New York, 1938), pp. 25–36. Reprinted by permission of Columbia University Press.

obliquely from its first line of direction. The people may err in their choice; but common interest and common sentiment are rarely mistaken.

Repelling all suggestions for a change in the parliamentary franchise, he supported the thesis —

that neither now nor at any time is it prudent or safe to be meddling with the fundamental principles and ancient tried usages of our constitution—that our representation is as nearly perfect as the necessary imperfection of human affairs and of human creatures will suffer it to be. . . .

Similar views were continually expressed by those who opposed the Reform Bill of 1832. Even the nomination boroughs, said Peel, were a worthy feature of the ancient constitution, because they permitted the ablest representatives of the national interests to be returned as a matter of course. And anyone with sufficient curiosity to search the parliamentary debates can find the same reasoning employed on many other occasions.

Much earlier, though without Burke's support, the British government had declared that the American complaint of taxation without representation was ill-founded: the colonists, it was true, elected no deputies to parliament: yet they were as adequately represented as most Englishmen. Not very long ago the women were still being told that they had no real need of the suffrage, for the men represented them better than they could hope to represent themselves. Attacking the Parliament Bill of 1911, the Duke of Northumberland denounced the house of commons as a body of paid politicians and proclaimed the house of lords "the most independent assembly in the world." Said he: "We represent, my lords, in a peculiar degree the education and the intelligence of the country."

Here, obviously, lies the trouble with Burke's argument. It can be used, not merely, as he used it, to defend aristocratic control of the commons, but to justify any regime that the speaker happens to like. May not Hitler assert that, by virtue of a "sympathy in feelings and desires," he represents the German people? Perhaps he has asserted it; and yet others will disagree. Indeed, any government, according to the personal attitude of the critic, may in this way be said to represent or not to represent the governed. On ultimate analysis virtual representation proves to be at its best a somewhat impractical ideal, at its worst a mere figure of speech. And in any case it is not what we normally understand as representative government. In dealing with the beginnings of the latter — as in this paper — we must keep our eyes on actual representation, that is, the practice of electing and commissioning deputies.

Accordingly, I must differ with those who, for the present subject of inquiry, find significance in the fact that the hundred court was anciently called the hundred, and the county court the county. The usage, in my opinion, hardly implies a true theory of representation. Does it not merely reflect the popular identification of a community with its government — as when we say that Russia declared war, that the church forbade the marriage of priests, or that a city regulated traffic? The language suggests at most a lawful spokesman. Nor can I, with Mr. McIlwain, perceive a germ of modern representative institutions in another practice of medieval courts: that of having a body of doomsmen or *scabini*[1] to declare the customary law. Since they were not elected by the suitors, they could have been representatives only in a figurative sense.

More to the point is a famous passage in the *Leges Henrici Primi*. These so-called Laws of Henry I state that the demesnes of a lord may, in either the county or the hundred court, be acquitted by the lord or his steward or, if they are

[1] In Teutonic pre-feudal societies, the *scabini* were older men of the community who sat on the local court and answered questions about the details of customary law. [Editor's note.]

of necessity absent, by the reeve, the priest, and four of the better men of the vill, on behalf of all who are not summoned by name. From that dubious assertion by a private compiler of the twelfth century, illumined by an ardent faith in the self-governing township, the Germanist school of historians once deduced a primeval English constitution based on the representative principle. Writing on the common meeting of the free Teutonic villagers, John Richard Green eloquently expressed the conviction of Freeman, Stubbs, and virtually their entire generation:

Here new settlers were admitted to the freedom of the township, and bye-laws framed and headman and tithing-man chosen for its governance. Here plough-land and meadowland were shared in due lot among the villagers, and field and homestead passed from man to man by the delivery of a turf cut from its soil. Here strife of farmer with farmer was settled according to the "customs" of the township as its elder men stated them, and four men were chosen to follow headman or ealdorman to hundred court or war. It is with a reverence such as is stirred by the sight of the headwaters of some mighty river that one looks back to these village moots. . . . It was here that England learned to be a "mother of parliaments."

That such an idyllic picture had to be blotted out by a new generation of scholars is indeed a pity. Even one in our own midst, Mr. Charles Beard, has shown himself especially ruthless. Sympathizing with those who wish to save a corner of that once lovely fabric, I yet fear it is gone beyond hope of restoration. Mr. McIlwain would have us believe that the *Leges Henrici Primi* sketch a representative system which at least in part was Anglo-Saxon. To me as to Mr. Beard, however, the passage in question does not portray a scheme of local representative government at all. In the appearance for the vill of the reeve, priest, and four select villeins, the anonymous author seems to be describing — for he is chronically inaccurate — an occa-

sional procedure, such as that adopted for the Domesday inquest of 1086. The reference, in other words, is not to an ancient routine of administering justice in shire and hundred, but to a Norman adaptation of the jury.

Here, at last, we reach something fairly solid; an opinion touching the origin of the English representative system becomes less an act of faith, as it was with Stubbs, and more a matter of real understanding. And in this connection we are all greatly indebted to Mr. A. B. White. He has convincingly shown that the characteristic self-government of the English people was due rather to the training of their Norman-French kings than to "an urge . . . in Anglo-Saxon blood." The principal stages of the development, as he sees it, are already familiar to students of English constitutional history. In the course of the twelfth century, local juries came to be used more and more frequently for a great variety of governmental business: to secure information concerning the privileges of individuals or communities; to assess persons and estates for maintenance of arms or payment of taxes; to bring charges against dishonest officials; to present the names of suspected criminals; to settle disputed titles to land or other property; to answer all sorts of questions put by the royal justices on eyre. Not uncommonly the desired results could best be obtained when the juries were popularly elected, and occasionally it was found convenient to call together a number of juries to consult with the king or his ministers. In the later thirteenth century such assemblies came to be associated with meetings of the great council; and so, we are told, the house of commons ultimately emerged.

At this point, however, I should like to interpose another distinction: that between a jury system and a system of representative government. The one does not inevitably imply the other. The essence of a jury was not that certain men were elected to represent others, but merely that certain men were put on oath to give true answers to questions. Two hundred years after the Norman Conquest the jury remained primarily a fact-finding institution. What was still demanded of the juror was particular knowledge, rather than authority to act on behalf of a community. So long as the king merely wanted information, a system of appointed juries, consulted either singly or in groups, would be entirely adequate. This may be representative government of a sort, but it is not what we recognize by that name in later England.

Sometimes, indeed, it was necessary for juries to be popularly elected — as when the counties were asked to present complaints of official maladministration. Also, when the royal justices made their great eyres through the country, they presumably wanted the juries from the local communities to be free of dictation on the part of sheriffs or bailiffs, and so encouraged a form of popular choice. In any case, there can be no doubt that by 1250 elected deputies of county, hundred, borough, or manor were often being called on for help in assessing and collecting taxes. And by that time the greater towns had formal rights of self-government, with elected magistrates and municipal councils. It is clear, therefore, that representative institutions were more than a by-product of the jury system. They were, in fact, more than a result of convenience in royal administration. To explain their new prominence in the thirteenth century, the economic and social developments of the age must be taken into account.

From this point of view the assembly of 1254 is especially significant, and it was not a mere concentration of juries. In February of that year the king commanded the election in each county court of two lawful and discreet knights, to come before the royal council at Westminster and there represent all and several of the county in granting him an aid for his expedition to France. The sheriff was to explain to the knights and others of the county the urgency of the king's needs and was to induce them to render an efficacious aid, so that the elected knights could make a precise response to the council. For the first time, so far as we can tell, knights of the shires were then summoned to attend parliament. Also for the first time, as Mr. J. G. Edwards has remarked, such deputies were required to bear what amounted to powers of attorney from their respective counties.

An authorization of the sort demanded in 1254 was no empty formula; it bound the whole county to the specific action taken by its delegates. And a very similar requirement was placed in the writs of 1268 for the election of burgesses to come before the king and council — the earliest such writs of which we have the complete wording. Indeed, the record contains the actual form of the letters to be sealed and attested by the electing community:

To all faithful in Christ before whom these present letters shall come, the mayor, bailiffs, and entire community of the city of York, greeting in the Lord. For the sake of the affairs concerning our lord king H[enry], illustrious king of England, his kingdom, the community of England, and us [to be considered], in the council called by the legate at London on the approaching quinzime of Easter, we have seen fit to send thither ——, our mayor, and ——, our bailiffs, and ——, our citizens or fellow burgesses, so that full faith may be given to them in everything which, with regard to the aforesaid matters, they shall see fit on our behalf to set forth in the council or on the occasion of the council. And we shall hold as established and accepted whatever on our behalf those men do in the aforesaid matters. In testimony whereof, etc. Given, etc.

The precedents thus set under Henry III were continuously followed under Edward I. Almost every writ that he issued for the election to parliament of burgesses or knights of the shires includes a provision that the men so chosen must have binding authority to act on behalf of their communities. For a score of years there was considerable variation in the phrases used; then the formula was invented that continued in official use for over five hundred years:

. . . We command and firmly enjoin you that without delay you cause two knights, of the more discreet and more capable of labor, to be elected from the aforesaid county, and two citizens from each city of the aforesaid county, and two burgesses from each borough, and that you have them come to us on the day and at the place aforesaid; so that the said knights shall then and there have full and sufficient authority on behalf of themselves and the community of the county aforesaid, and the said citizens and burgesses on behalf of themselves and the respective communities of the cities and boroughs aforesaid, to do whatever in the aforesaid matters may be ordained by common counsel; and so that, through default of such authority, the aforesaid business shall by no means remain unfinished. . . .

I heartily agree with Mr. Edwards that this is a fact deserving greater attention than it has hitherto received. Why was the king so insistent, not only upon the election of lawful men from county and borough, but also upon their being formally empowered to bind their constituents? Surely he must have wanted more than information, complaints, or requests. Within the last quarter of a century, for all the modern emphasis on economic factors in history, many writers on parliamentary origins have stressed judicial routine as the dominating influence in the development of both houses. Against that opinion I registered a mild protest in 1929. Now, after a wider reading of the pertinent evidence, I am prepared to strengthen it. The crux of the matter, it seems to me, lies in the distinction — the third and final one of this paper — between the original functions of parliament and the original functions of the commons in parliament.

The research of Messrs. Richardson and Sayles has proved in detail that under the three Edwards the main business of parliament continued to be judicial. Most of the work that later devolved upon the privy council or the chancellor — the settlement of cases lying beyond the jurisdiction of the common law courts — was still in the fourteenth century handled by parliament. But this body, the greatest and highest of the king's courts, was the original parliament, in which burgesses and knights of the shire had no place. In 1400 the commons set forth to the newly enthroned Henry IV —

that, whereas the judgments of parliament pertained solely to the king and to the lords, and not to the commons except in case it pleased the king of his special grace to show them the same judgments for their satisfaction, no record should be made in parliament concerning the said commons to the effect that they are or shall be parties to any judgments henceforth to be given in parliament. To which, at the king's command, response was made by the archbishop of Canterbury, to the effect that the commons are petitioners and demandants and that the king and the lords have always had and of right shall have the [rendering of] judgments in parliament after the manner described by the same commons; except that the king especially wishes to have their advice and assent in the making of statutes, or of grants and subsidies, or [other] such matters for the common good of the realm.

The action thus taken merely confirmed the established custom of England. The commons were not and never had been judges in parliament. The fact that meetings of the parliament had come to be associated with meetings of deputies from the local communities had, so far as judicial work was concerned, no legal significance. In the words of Mr. H. L. Gray,

The century of the three Edwards remains one during which the commons were practically non-existent for any one who wished to offer a petition in parliament. They stood in the same position as did the petitioner himself.

If, therefore, we take judicial functions as the determining factor in the rise of the commons, we are reduced to the contention that they were somehow invaluable as petitioners. It is, of course, undeniable that before the time of Edward I meetings of deputies were sometimes held for the specific purpose of recording popular grievances, and that in a few of the later parliaments the commons apparently did nothing but present petitions. As acutely remarked by Mr. Richardson, however,

the real problem . . . is not to explain the occasional association of popular representation with a session of parliament in England or elsewhere, but to explain why popular representation became an essential and inseparable feature of English parliaments. The explanation is not to be found by any examination of the origins of parliament, however far-reaching or ingenious.

Neither, I would add, is it to be found by tracing into earlier times any political practice that did not involve the actual election of deputies with a delegation of binding authority from the communities of England. The assembling of such communal representatives apparently began in 1254 and developed into a regular custom by the end of the century. Why a king like Edward I should have insisted on these assemblies merely to facilitate the presentation of petitions I cannot understand. But I can understand how the bringing of petitions in parliament would be encouraged by the constant election of burgesses and knights of the shires for other purposes. The principal purpose, I am convinced, was to obtain money — a conclusion that agrees with the known character of the king and the social and economic changes of the age.

The euphemistic language of the royal writs should not mislead us. In 1241 Henry III called at Worcester an assembly of the wealthier Jews from all his boroughs *ad tractandum nobiscum tam de nostra quam sua utilitate* [to treat with us for our benefit as well as theirs]. But the matter of mutual advantage of which they were to treat was actually a tallage of 20,000 marks. When Edward I notified his good men of various towns that he had commissioned John of Kirkby to explain to them and expedite through them "certain arduous and especial concerns" of his, no one could have been surprised to discover that he was negotiating for a subsidy. And contemporaries were as little mystified when parliamentary representatives were summoned to consider those other "difficult and momentous affairs" to which the writs constantly refer. They knew that they would be fortunate to escape further demands for taxes.

Mr. McIlwain goes so far as to remark that, if we confine our attention to the innovations affecting parliament under Henry III, "the contemporary evidence is strongly in favour of Bishop Stubbs' view that the original motive behind the beginning of these changes was almost entirely fiscal." To my mind the evidence for a similar motive on the part of Edward I is even stronger. On reëxamining the records of his sixteen parliaments that included deputations of the commons, Miss M. V. Clarke has found only three in which no question of a grant was apparently raised. "The evolution of the *premunientes* [securing (full and sufficient power)] clause . . . to bring the proctors of the clergy to parliament," she points out, "was frankly fiscal in intention, as there was no other reason why Edward I should require their presence." And it seems idle to assert that the king had the right to tax the freeholders of shire and borough at will. As a matter of fact, the royal tallage on the towns had normally been levied through negotiation with the individual communities, and in the later thirteenth century the tallage was generally supplanted by subsidies officially styled free. Meanwhile, as the burden of taxation was shifted downward from the barons to their knightly tenants, it had become practically imperative for the king to seek formal grants from the county courts according to the plan adopted in 1254.

When, under Edward III, the proceedings of parliament come to be entered in the rolls, they offer continuous proof that the primary task of the commons was to vote supply. The reader almost invariably knows what to expect at the opening session. After the usual preliminaries, the lord chancellor, or some other minister, would explain the reasons for the calling of the parliament. He would set forth the great expense incurred by the king in defending the realm, in promoting worthy projects abroad, in repressing civil disorder, in maintaining the regal estate, and in otherwise assuring to the English people the blessings of a sound administration; so, in the face of the existing emergency, he would urge the commons to make generous provision for his majesty's needs, promising a gracious consideration of whatever requests they might care to make. And it is a very familiar story how the commons, by formulating joint petitions and stipulating royal approval as the necessary condition to a grant of supply, ultimately established their control over the vital functions of the government.

Accordingly, if the view here expressed is justified, the core of the English representative system has not been a vague sympathy on the part of self-appointed spokesmen, a primitive custom of deeming dooms in the name of the people, or even the selection of jurors for a sort of national inquest. Rather it has been a matter of sheer political necessity, occasioned on the one hand by the king's lack of money and on the other by the growing strength of the social groups who could supply it. Although the king might use communal delegates in a variety of ways, the compelling motive behind their incorporation as an estate of parliament was economic. Without the recurring need for general taxation, there would, I believe, have been no house of commons.

In concluding, it may also be remarked that some of the constitutional features praised by Burke as "the ancient tried usages" of England were by no means so fundamental as he imagined. It was not the original practice for members of the commons to be representatives of the nation at large. Actually, the burgesses and knights of the shires were procurators of the local communities, chosen and instructed by them, responsible to them, and legally bound to be resident within them. Contemporary political thought, of course, embraced no theory of democracy founded on universal suffrage. But it did recognize the interdependence of representation and popular election and, the principle of the mandate was not wholly foreign — all good Tories to the contrary notwithstanding.

# The Representatives as "Vessels of Power"

## SIR JOHN GORONWY EDWARDS

In the concluding part of his *Historians and the Medieval English Parliament*, cited below, Sir J. G. Edwards cautions against the current tendency to "write down" the role of parliamentary representatives.

THE REPRESENTATIVES with whom we are here concerned do not include the representatives of the diocesan clergy: we are concerned here only with the representatives of shires and cities and boroughs — two knights from each shire, and two citizens or burgesses from each city or borough. Each shire and city and borough was in law a *communitas*, a *commune*, i.e. it was an organic, quasi-corporate body. Each pair of representatives was treated in law as representing the whole community of the shire or city or borough from which they came. In order to stress this point, it was the rule from 1294 onwards to prescribe in the writs of summons that these representatives were to come to parliament bearing "full power" from their respective communities to do what should be ordered by common counsel in parliament, and the writs emphasized the legal importance of this "full power" by specifically saying that the representatives must have it "so that the business may not remain unachieved for lack of such power." The representatives received expenses from their constituencies, calculated at so much per day for the time they spent in parliament, *plus* a reasonable and specific number of days for travelling there and back. As the writs for the payment of these expenses as well as the election returns have survived in large numbers, we have a great deal of information about the names of the persons who were chosen as representatives, and a good deal also about the length of time that they spent in the parliaments which they attended. But we are much less fully informed about what they did while they were there. We can indeed see pretty clearly that during the course of a parliament the representatives often spent a good deal of the time holding discussions among themselves in a room apart where, as a fourteenth-century chronicler put it, they could "take counsel privily without being disturbed or worried by other persons": when parliament met at Westminster, the Commons held their discussions, at times in the Painted Chamber of the royal palace, at times in the chapter house, and at times in the refectory of the abbey. We can also know the purport of any discussion among the commons if — as occurred not infrequently — its outcome happened to be recorded on the parliament roll. But the parliament roll was not intended to be a record, still less a journal, of the proceedings of the Commons, and the view that it gives us of their proceedings in their own room — or "house," as it was being called by the beginning of the fifteenth century — is not an unrestricted view, but rather a series of partial glimpses seen as it were through chinks in a closed door. The result is that the evidence about the doings of the representatives in the medieval English parliament has at different times been very variously interpreted.

William Prynne, the pioneer of English parliamentary history, was himself a dis-

From Sir J. G. Edwards, *Historians and the Medieval English Parliament* (Glasgow, 1960), pp. 24–42. Reprinted by permission of Jackson, Son and Company and of the author.

tinguished member of the house of commons of his day — he began his parliamentary career in the Long Parliament and was one of those excluded by Pride's Purge — so he naturally wrote about the representatives rather proudly, and left no doubt that he regarded them as having been "a good thing." This traditional tone continued into the nineteenth century, when it is well exemplified, for instance, in the writings of Freeman and of Stubbs. But during the last sixty or seventy years there has been an unmistakable and growing tendency among some scholars, if not actually to write the medieval representatives *off*, at any rate very definitely to write them *down*. This has happened partly by sheer reaction against traditional views as such, and partly by reflection of the general spirit of the age, which no longer regards representative government as being axiomatically "a good thing." But it has happened partly also as a concomitant of the doctrine that the essential function of parliament was "the dispensing of justice," and that its other functions could be "stripped away" as "non-essential": to the extent that this doctrine has been accepted, attention has been deflected away from the representatives, and the significance of representation in the medieval English parliament has been minimized accordingly.

This general tendency has been variously exemplified. An early symptom of it was the theory, put forward in the eighteen-eighties, that representatives were added to parliament by Edward I not, as the traditional doctrine had stated, in order that they might give consent to taxation, but rather in order that they might act as the king's collectors in gathering the taxation to which they had assented. Again, because borough constituencies were quite often returned by the sheriff as having made "no answer" to the mandate ordering them to elect representatives, it was supposed that this "no answer" meant that no election was made, and that many constituencies thus evaded representation by the simple expedient of omitting to elect.

This vein of thought was rapidly opened up still further. The assumption was made that representatives who had been elected to any given parliament, but for whom no writ of expenses was enrolled, could probably be regarded (by and large) as having absented themselves from that parliament. As no expenses are enrolled for a great many representatives — particularly of boroughs — known to have been elected, it was inferred that many parliamentary representatives evaded their duties by the simple expedient of omitting to attend. Again, because it seemed that representatives were "rarely re-elected," and because the sessions of medieval parliaments were seldom very long and were often quite short, it was inferred that even the representatives who were re-elected and who did trouble to attend would still have no adequate opportunity of gaining any effective experience of parliament, or much personal acquaintance with their fellow-representatives from other constituencies.

All this had at least the practical utility of being provocative, and although further discussion showed that much of it was rather hasty, it did in the long run have the substantial merit of drawing attention to some aspects of historical truth which had been, or easily might be, overlooked. It was, however, hasty to suppose that Edward I summoned representatives in order that they might act as collectors of the taxes granted in parliament: Pasquet subsequently pointed out that such a theory would apply to only a fraction of the shire representatives, and not at all to the representatives of the boroughs. Again, it was hasty to suppose, because many borough constituencies were from time to time returned by the sheriff as having made "no answer," that they therefore made no election: there are examples which show that boroughs which were returned as having made "no answer" did nevertheless make an election as ordered; in such cases, all that the sheriff meant when he returned a borough as having made "no answer" was that it had made no answer *up to the time when he was making his return.* On the other hand, it is undoubtedly true that some boroughs (and occasionally even shires) did from time to time desire to avoid representation in order to save the expense of paying the representatives' wages.

It was still more hasty to suppose that the writs of expenses recorded in the Close Rolls give anything like complete lists of the representatives who actually attended the various parliaments: in parliament after parliament we have examples of representatives who are known to have been present, but for whom nevertheless no writs *de expenses* are enrolled. There is no longer any doubt that the number of representatives actually attending parliaments was much greater than the number for whom writs of expenses are enrolled on the Close Rolls. Prynne long ago realised that this was the position, and repeatedly said so.

Again it was, if not hasty, at any rate very misleading, to say that representatives were "rarely re-elected." "Re-elected" can mean one of two things. In the strictest sense it means that a person is elected to two or more immediately successive parliaments. In the more general sense it means that a person is elected to two or more parliaments, whether or not they are immediately successive. In the strictest sense of the word, the statement that the representatives were rarely "re-elected" is broadly quite true. In the more general sense of the word "re-elected," the statement is completely untrue: from a very early stage in the history of the representative parliament in England we find an appreciable and growing number of representatives who were elected repeatedly and who in fact attended parliament repeatedly. Medieval English representative parliaments contained, almost from the first, an appreciable and growing number of representatives who had some previous experience of parliament and of whatever may have been its traditional procedure, and some previous acquaintance with their fellow representatives — for whatever that experience and acquaintance may have been worth. At the same time, it is true that a very considerable number — quite possibly the majority — of the persons elected as parliamentary representatives during the medieval period were elected only once. Such, then, is the position: "an appreciable and growing number of representatives were elected repeatedly"; "most probably the majority were elected only once." Both statements are true. Neither may be neglected. Only when taken together do they establish the whole truth. It is this: that although the greater *number of representatives* consisted of those elected only once, yet the greater *amount of representation* was supplied by those elected repeatedly.

For the reasons stated it therefore seems fair to say that the tendency to cry down the representatives in medieval English parliaments — to argue that many constituencies omitted to elect representatives; that many representatives who were elected omitted to attend; that those who did attend gained little effective parliamentary "experience"; and that anyhow their parliamentary "experience" was largely barren because they were "rarely re-elected" — is a tendency that has been well-marked rather than well-founded.

The particular and technical issues of election, "re-election," attendance and "experience" are ultimately of interest, however, not so much for their own sake as for their bearing upon a question that is more general. It may be stated thus: what influence was exerted by the representatives in the working of medieval English parliaments? The inherent difficulties of this question are well illustrated by one of the more recent answers to it that have been proposed, an answer which has been conveniently summarized in the following passage:

It is generally stated that, because the Commons [i.e. the representatives in parliament] included within their ranks many county gentry, trained in unpaid public services, lawyers, business men, and experienced parliamentarians, they exerted a great influence in parliament. Yet this is a mere assumption: if it were true, then we should expect to find it borne out by the evidence. But, on the contrary, the facts point to the subservience rather than the independence of the Commons. For in all questions of high politics the direction came from the lords.

It is in fact very doubtful whether the view that the representatives "exerted a great influence" in medieval parliaments is a proposition that "is generally stated," at any rate by historians during the last forty or fifty years. But even if such a proposition were "generally stated," its implications would obviously depend very much upon the interpretation given to the phrase "exerting a great influence in parliament." In the passage just quoted, "exerting a great influence in parliament" is taken to mean acting with "independence" in "all questions of high politics." Now that criterion, although in itself quite reasonable, is one that is neither equally relevant nor equally applicable to every period in the history of parliament. It is really relevant only in those periods when "high politics" were a frequently recurring subject of parliamentary concern. It is effectively applicable only in those periods for which appropriate evidence is available. Sir John Neale and Sir Lewis Namier have described and estimated in some detail the kinds and degrees of influence that the representatives exerted upon "high politics" in English parliaments under Elizabeth I and in British parliaments under George III. They have been able to do so, not only because parliament in those reigns was very frequently involved in "high politics," but also because they could draw upon numerous direct records of the representatives' debates, and upon considerable masses of other material like letters and diaries which throw light upon the relations that existed between the men who were then concerned with politics and with parliament. In the medieval period, however, parliament was not in-

volved in "high politics" with anything like the same frequency as under Elizabeth I and George III. And even for the occasions when it was so involved, appropriate evidence is lamentably deficient. Such things as letters and diaries are entirely lacking or extremely scrappy. As for the representatives' debates, there is only one solitary document which purports to be a direct record of them: that unique report is fortunately preserved in the *Anonimalle Chronicle* of St. Mary's, York, and its uniqueness gives it great interest, but it provides no more than a short summary of just a few of the representatives' discussions in a single parliament, the "Good Parliament" of 1376. So whether the "assumption" be that the medieval parliamentary representatives exerted a great influence or a small influence "in all questions of high politics," the one thing that we can hardly "expect" is to find either assumption "borne out by the evidence" — borne out, that is, in any convincing way — for the simple reason that the only kinds of evidence which could bear it out at all cogently are not available, and quite possibly have never even existed. Moreover, although the medieval English parliament did — *on occasion* — become involved in "high politics," it was also involved — not merely on occasion, but constantly — in politics that were not "high" and in matters that were hardly "politics." Whether the representatives "exerted a great influence" in medieval parliaments therefore depends only in part upon their role in "high politics": it depends at least equally, and quite probably a great deal more, upon their role in parliamentary business other than "high politics." So even if it were established by cogent evidence that "in all questions of high politics the direction came from the lords" and that in the handling of those questions the Commons were "subservient," such a conclusion would still leave entirely unresolved the problem of the influence which the representatives exerted in the more frequented sphere of parliamentary business below the plane of "high politics." Their influence in that sphere has not as yet been satisfactorily appraised. The evidence on the point is admittedly very difficult to interpret. But evidence does at least exist, and it exists — such as it is — in quite considerable quantities.

Whatever may have been the part played by the representatives — whether in "high politics" or in other matters — in medieval parliaments, any estimate of it must from the start take account of one general and overriding consideration. There is no doubt that the adding of representatives to the English parliament was resorted to only as an occasional expedient during the last quarter of the thirteenth century; there is no doubt that it grew into an established practice during the first quarter of the fourteenth. Since the representatives thus became fixtures in parliament in the course of some two generations, we are driven to suppose that the part which they played in parliament was at any rate sufficiently significant to have seemed worth while to both the parties involved, that is, to the king and his ministers on the one hand, and to the representatives and their constituencies on the other.

If we regard things from the standpoint of the Government, we may reasonably conclude that, in some significant sense or senses, the summoning of the representatives appeared to kings and their ministers to have been worth while, otherwise we could hardly suppose that such busy personages would have gone on burdening themselves and their subordinates with all the additional complexities involved in the summoning and provisioning and holding of parliaments that were representative, or that they would have gone on burdening the local communities with the paying of the representatives' expenses. I have said "kings and their ministers" for a particular reason. One of the more fruitful sides of the doctrine that the essence of

parliament was the dispensing of justice has been its incidental emphasis upon the important part played by the king's ministers and counsellors in the working and development of parliament, particularly under Edward I: "their contribution," it has been said, "was immeasureably greater than that of any other body of men represented there." The proposition is broadly true, provided always we bear in mind that one of the very important "contributions" which royal ministers and counsellors made to parliament, not merely under Edward I but also under his son and grandson, was to continue advising the king to continue summoning the representatives. For we may not safely suppose that an institution like the representative parliament of England was something which came into being entirely or even predominantly on the personal initiative of kings: it was something begun, continued and established by kings, acting throughout with the counsel and active collaboration of ministers. During the period when parliament sometimes included representatives and sometimes did not, and when therefore the summoning of the representatives was not yet settled by routine, the chancery clerks who issued the writs of summons would presumably need to be instructed when the representatives were to be included: in other words, the summoning of the representatives, so long as it was not a matter of course, would require a specific decision in each case. Constitutional historians would give a great deal to possess some medieval record of the procedure — and especially of any discussions — by which such decisions were reached, but no record of that kind seems to exist. That such decisions would be made in the circle of the king's counsellors might be expected on general grounds, and in fact there is at least one piece of specific though indirect evidence to that effect. A parliament was summoned to meet at York on 8 February 1310 by writs dated 26 October 1309. At that time Edward II was sojourning in the north of England. On 4 November 1309, in the course of a letter to the earl of Lincoln, the king remarks that he had decided to summon this assembly, which he refers to as "our great parliament," "par nostre conseil qe nous avioms a Everwyk." To that "great parliament," as it happens, representatives were probably not summoned, but if they had been, the decision would doubtless have been likewise reached by Edward II "par nostre conseil qe nous avioms a Everwyk," i.e. after consulting with somebody or other among the officers and counsellors who were in attendance upon him at York. In such consultations, there was at least as much room for ministerial as for royal initiative.

If we regard things from the standpoint of the representatives — a standpoint not always taken sufficiently into account — we may reasonably conclude that, in some significant sense or senses, going to parliament appeared to the representatives themselves, and to the constituencies who paid their expenses, to be a proceeding that was at least intelligible. Its intelligibility was at any rate a subject on which the representatives had much opportunity for hard thinking, and for thinking hard things. When they went to parliament, they were not borne thither comfortably somnolent in railway carriages. They

rode upon their rouncies as they couthe,

and if as they rode they were ever sleepy, it would be mostly from cold and from weariness of their riding. For medieval parliaments did not most commonly assemble

Whan Zephirus eek with his swete breeth
Inspired hath in every holt and heeth
The tendre croppes, and the yonge sonne
Hath in the Ram his halfe cours yronne.

More often they were called for October or November or January or February, when it's

Hey, ho, the wind and the rain

and

When icicles hang by the wall.

Yet the riding to parliament persisted. So the part which the riders played on arrival presumably seemed *to them themselves* to be worth their playing. Modern historians may quite easily so disparage the part played by medieval parliamentary representatives that the very fact of medieval parliamentary representation is made largely unintelligible.

It seems, then, that if we are to understand the medieval English parliament as it really was, we must regard it as having been in origin not "a high court of justice," not a high court *of* anything, but simply a high court. The medieval king, in England as in some places elsewhere, was deemed to act always (as the phrase went) "with counsel." Sometimes, indeed, that counsel might be regarded as "evil counsel," but good or evil it was "with counsel" that the king was deemed to act. In England it was in parliament that the king found counsel at its amplest, so it was in parliament that his power was legally at its highest. That was why parliament was a "high court" and why king in parliament was omnicompetent. Such was the essence of the pre-representative parliament in England. To it the king and his ministers added the representatives of shires and boroughs. These representatives enlarged the existing amplitude of parliament with a new amplitude because, humble vessels though they were, yet legally they were vessels of power: the king commanded them to bring — and they duly brought — to parliament from the local communities of shire and borough a *potestas* that was called *plena*. This "full power" was, as the solitary chronicler who mentions the summoning of representatives duly points out, a "potestas obligandi comitatum, et faciendi quod per consilium regis ordinaretur" [power to bind the county and to do what the king shall ordain through his counsel]. This fusion of the omnicompetence of the pre-representative parliament with the full power of the representatives to "obligate" the local communities persisted beneath the "drums and tramplings" of five centuries, and thereby provided the groundwork of ideas for that doctrine of parliamentary sovereignty which became, from a legal point of view, "the dominant characteristic of English political institutions."

# III. ENGLISH REPRESENTATIVE PARLIAMENTS AND THEIR EUROPEAN COUNTERPARTS: WHO INFLUENCED WHOM?

## The Dominicans and Representation

### HENRY PORTER TUNMORE

Henry Porter Tunmore (1916– ), a Harvard graduate, spent much of his post-college career with the United States government; in the Department of State during World War II and, subsequently, in the Department of Defense. Since 1956, he has served as an Information Officer with the United Nations in New York. In the selection below, taken from an article in the *Catholic Historical Review* in 1941, Tunmore evaluates Sir Ernest Barker's thesis concerning the contributions of the Dominicans to the development of representative practices in thirteenth-century England.

DURING THE THIRTEENTH CENTURY over approximately the same space of years representation, as a principle of government, was adopted by the Dominican Order and by the English parliament. St. Dominic drew up the preliminary organization of his Order in 1216, an Order based initially on the rule of St. Augustine, and in the same year he secured papal approval. In 1220 the first Chapter General meeting at Bologna adopted the "constitutiones" which laid down the permanent legislative and representative structure of the Order. In 1221 Prior Gilbert of Fresney brought a colony of Dominicans to Oxford. Five years later Stephen Langton, archbishop of Canterbury, a good friend and patron of the Oxford friars, applied the representative principle to the convocations of the English Church. By 1273 Robert Kilwardby, the Dominican archbishop of Canterbury, was extending this same principle by calling up proctors from each diocese to convocation.

Simultaneously the representative principle conceived nationally was appearing in the King's Council or parliament. King John issued a writ in 1213 summoning four knights from every shire to appear at a great council to discuss "the affairs of our kingdom." So far as we know, this parliament never met. In 1254 Henry III called up four knights of the shire from all over the realm and these county delegates actually did meet to discuss granting money to the king. Another writ in 1261 called up the knights again, this time to discuss "the common affairs of our realm." In 1265 Simon de Montfort held his own parliament at London and called up, now for the first time, both knights of the shire and burgesses from the towns. The practice was probably continued more or less regularly after de Montfort's parliament, for

From H. P. Tunmore, "The Dominican Order and Parliament," *Catholic Historical Review*, XXVI (1941), pp. 479–488. Reprinted by permission of The Catholic University of America Press.

Edward I's writ summoning knights and burgesses in 1275 makes it clear that he was following precedents.

Put side by side in this way these events in the Dominican Order and in parliament easily set us wondering. What connection, if any, is there between the two series of happenings? Did parliament introduce national representatives after the example of the Dominicans? Did both parliament and the Dominicans take the principle from a common source? The third possibility — that the Dominicans copied parliament — we can count out. If the first national representatives did not sit in parliament until 1254, it is clear that their example could not have influenced an organization practically complete in 1220.

The problems involved in giving a clear, full answer to these questions are far from being simple. Expert scholars disagree. Some of the essential sources have hardly been touched. Not a single whole volume has yet been written on the subject. For these reasons I can do little more than discuss the subject in terms of its sources, the general historical background, and an accurate understanding of the problems that lie behind the question: what is the connection between the Dominicans and parliament? My task must be to describe what the student must do, not to set down incomplete investigations. . . .

In a letter dated November 17, 1205, Innocent III gratified his friend, Dominic of Osma, by creating the Apostolic Friars, a fraternity composed of the religious whom St. Dominic had gathered round him. This was to be a type of preachers patterned after the Gospels. In the same year St. Dominic founded the monastery of Prouille, Toulouse, which was to follow the Rule of St. Augustine. He gave them his own "Institutions" as a guide for the spiritual and temporal administration of the individual convent. The Order of Friars Preachers with its rule and Dominic's "Consuetudines" was formally approved in 1216 by a papal bull. These "Consuetu-dines" of 1216 regulated the ascetic and canonical life of the new order. The "Constitutiones" of 1220, drawn up at the first general chapter in Bologna, regulated the political organization of the Order, laying down (as Mandonnet says) "the essential and original basis of Dominican legislation."

The Order was to be governed under its Constitution by the general chapter, meeting annually, and the master-general, elected by the provincial priors and two brothers from each province. His term in the thirteenth century and throughout the Middle Ages was for life. The master general was and is the chief administrator. From his residence in Rome he visited the provinces, saw to it that the laws of the Order were observed, corrected abuses. The general chapter was the supreme legislative authority. It made new laws ("constitutiones"), discussed any current legislative or disciplinary business. It corrected the master-general and had the power to depose him under certain circumstances.

"Our Order," says the Constitution, "was instituted principally for preaching and the salvation of souls." (Version of 1228). This motivating principle was carried out in the whole frame of the Order, showing itself especially in the provision of a doctor of theology to lecture in every convent, in the sending of preachers on tour and in the exemption of the friars from manual labor.

The structure of the Order rested on the convent as on a cell and rose up through the province to the Order, that is, to the provinces collectively considered. The prior, chosen by the brothers, was governor of the convent but he was obliged to consult the conventual chapter in most important matters. The province was ruled by the provincial prior and the provincial chapter, acting respectively as administrator and law-maker. In this intermediate chapter sat the provincial, the priors, a delegate from each convent and the "general preachers." Four members were regularly chosen to act as a committee for preparing legislation and discussion. The general chapter, a kind of supreme congress, met annually, being composed every two successive years of "definitores" or delegates (one from each province) and in the third year of provincial priors. A generalissimo chapter met twice in the history of the Order, both times in the thirteenth century. It seems to have been provided for in the "Constitutiones" as a quick method for getting laws passed. To become a law an "actum" had ordinarily to be passed by three successive general chapters. The generalissimo chapter, it can be seen, was really three general chapters meeting in one, for it is made up of *two* delegates from each province *and* all the provincials.

The main features of this structure were by no means all new, but the governing principle that informed them was quite new. As Dr. Galbraith has shown, the Dominican "constitutiones" of 1220 owed much to Prémontré. Like the Premonstratensians the Friar Preachers were to be Canons Regular. They were to be divided into provinces with provincial chapters and to be subject to an abbot-general. But St. Dominic remodeled both the province and the provincial chapter, making them units of government and not units of visitation merely. The master-general became a powerful administrator, not just a glorified visitor from the mother-house, but at the same time he was made responsible to the general chapter. The provincial priors and the priors, once elected, did not become autocrats but were also held responsible to their constituents. The chapters, not the officers, ruled. The change was even evident in the outward bearing of these new friars. They did not bow and prostrate themselves, the regular habit of the monks and of the Premonstratensians as well, but stood ever erect. St. Dominic had intended and seen to it that his Order should be ruled by its representatives. Here was a new principle, indeed.

The principle of representation, as it was appearing during these same years in the central government of England, was also a new thing. Yet it was not new in the sense that we are often assured of in the popular accounts. Many if not most historians who have written about the beginnings of representation in England describe these beginnings as if England was the *original* source of representative government. They are so impressed by the persistent growth of the House of Commons, by its survival coincident with the decline and disappearance of the continental cortes and états-généreaux, and by the current general acceptance of Parliament as the "mother of parliaments," that they forget altogether the Greek and Roman republics and the eleventh- and twelfth-century assemblies in Spain and Southern France.

According to this orthodox, English view, the beginnings of representation are to be found in the jury system practiced in the county courts all over mediaeval England. The Normans, borrowing from the Franks, brought the jury in its earliest form to England at the Conquest. Sworn men were required to appear in the county court they met there feudal freeholders, its owner and the rights of the king. When the king's travelling judges rode into this court they met there feudal freeholders, twelve burgesses from each borough or city, and a bailiff and four men from every village. The information asked of these juries gradually widened from questions about property to assessments for taxes and complaints against the sheriffs.

This English view has it that the change from the jury system to national representation in Parliament took place quite naturally and without attracting much attention. The king's travelling judges sometimes gave judgments which were refused by the county court. Such a court would then by order of the king send up four of its members to carry the judgment to the King's Court and there defend or attack it. Judicial committees of this kind went up to Westminster several times under Henry II, but ordinarily from one shire at a time. In 1226, however, four knights from eight counties met at Lincoln to hear complaints against their sheriffs. 1254 is usually hailed as a landmark in the development of representation, for in that year Henry III for the first time called up elected knights of the shire to ,a council for discussing non-judicial business. He wanted money in the form of an aid. The next major date is 1265 when Simon de Montfort summoned both knights and burgesses to his own great council.

E. M. Sait goes to much trouble to show where the English version of the rise of representation omits important facts (*Political Institutions*, Chap. 4). Simon de Montfort, it is true, summoned knights and burgesses for the first time in England in 1265, but there is strong evidence for believing that he had already done the same thing in Gascony where he was governor from 1246 to 1252. At any rate he was familiar with this kind of representation long before the great council of 1265. The "natural transition" from the judicial committees who went up to the King's Court in the early thirteenth century to the delegation of knights who discussed the royal money grant at the council of 1254 is actually pretty abrupt. The early committees who carried the county court records to Westminster never, so far as we know, had authority to deal with anything but judicial matter. Some other influence must have been added to make the king and his regents suddenly decide to let the Commoners talk over affairs of state. The king needed more money — yes — but what precedent could be shown to justify calling up plain Commoners to join with nobles and clergy? King John's writ of summons of 1213 to four knights from every shire is a still more serious obstacle to the paternal claim of the judicial committees. Where did John get the idea at a time when these committees had barely started going up to the King's Court?

The central question for the student is: what is the connection, if any, between the growth of representation in the Dominican Order and the almost simultaneous growth in Parliament or the King's Council? We have to remember that representation does not necessarily mean *control* by representatives. It exists wherever delegates *deliberate* or *decide* as the voice of the general will, whether it be the general will of a community, a social group or a whole nation. The thing that appears new about the Dominican Order, when we set it beside the already existing orders is the control that it allows the friars to exercise over their officers once those officers are elected. The thing that is new about the King's Council by 1275 is the acceptance of a *national* representation (*i.e.*, representation by a geographical unit instead of by feudal tenure) not indeed entitling the knights and burgesses to control the king but rather to deliberate ("ad tractandum" was the usual formula) such public matters as he presented to them. Although representation by geographical unit was not original with the Dominicans (the Canons of Piémontré practiced it) they gave the principle dramatic and vitalizing form in England. We must ask therefore whether Parliament owes anything to their example in this fundamental principle. We must also ask about the *new forms* of representation that the Dominicans introduced in this century — the use of elected committeemen to prepare legislation and discussion, the requirement of three readings to make an "actum" law, etc.

It may be questioned whether the word "growth" is really applicable to Dominican representation as a principle in this period. There were indeed important changes made in the "constitutiones" between 1228 and 1363, but these were for the most part changes defining and establishing on a sure basis the control of the respective chapters over the priors and the master-general. The "constitutiones" of 1220 brought into the world a practically full grown theory of representation. The elective amendments that were later introduced did not alter the essential structure. In the English state, however, there was a real growth evident between the summons for a money grant in 1254 and the preamble to the First Statute of Westminster, 1275. It may appear when more work has been done on the earlier period, that 1213 would be a better date to start the growth.

The two groups of historians writing to-day on the origins of English representation hold respectively to the notions of parallel development and diffusion. "Parallel development" is the theory we have already considered, the English theory that the development of representation in England in the thirteenth century, which finds a parallel development on the continent, can be understood without reference to that continental development. "Diffusion" means the belief that the changes which introduced a national representation into the thirteenth century English parliaments represent a spreading of the already existing institutions of Spain, Southern France and Sicily.

Professor Ernest Barker was the first important constitutional scholar to present a theory of diffusion. He saw that the advocate of diffusion would have to indicate a reasonable channel by which the representative customs of Spain and France reached England. His book, *The Dominican Order and Convocation* (1913), is an attempt to show that the Dominicans were that channel. He suggests that St. Dominic, himself a Spaniard, applied the representative principle of his people to his Order; that Stephen Langton, an important patron of the English Dominicans, applied this principle to the convocations of York and Canterbury; that the state borrowed it from the church; and that Simon de Montfort and Edward I, makers of the House of Commons, were influenced by Dominican counsellors.

Barker points to St. Dominic's background and early movements as important evidence for his thesis. St. Dominic, he reminds us, was a Canon of Osma in 1188, the probable date of the first representative "cortes" in Leon. Dominic would have been in a position to know thoroughly the customs of his people during the fifteen subsequent years in Leon. In 1203 he went from Osma to Southern France where he remained for ten years. During this time he met and became friendly with the elder Simon de Montfort, governor of Languedoc. In 1212 de Montfort convened a great parliament at Pamiers, to which, as was the custom in the local assemblies, delegates came from the towns. Perhaps St. Dominic was particularly impressed by this parliament when four years later he commenced the organization of the Order of Friar Preachers on a representative basis.

In 1221, Barker goes on to say, the first Dominicians landed in England. He then traces the development that we have already surveyed: the penetration into the universities and the King's Council, the eventual dominance of the new Order in political spheres. He insists that a Dominican or a friend of the Dominicans led at every stage in the growth of national representation.

When he comes to the council of 1254 with its knights of the shire Barker can point back to the convocation of 1226. Without giving more evidence he says, "Thirty years of the rule of Henry III are bearing fruit; and even if Boniface of Savoy is archbishop, the voice of the clergy will out and representation will come." Discussing de Montfort's great council of 1265 he admits that the summoning of knights and burgesses together may mean that de Montfort was copying "the institutions of Aragon, of Sicily, and of Gascony." He would have us remember, nevertheless, that the earl's father was a friend of St. Dominic, that the earl, himself, may have been taught by the friars, and that his wife found refuge and a burial among the Canonesses of St. Dominic at Montargis.

One fact Barker is hard put to reconcile with his theory. We know that King John was acquainted with the representative principle because he issued the writ of 1213. "But," answers Barker, "the events of 1226 are surely far more important than those of 1213, and the lesson they teach is the influence of the clergy on progress in political ideas." The ingenious argument he weaves from this point on cannot break the hard fact of 1213. As Sait says, "John actually summoned knights of the shire eight years before the Dominican Order, was organized, eight years before the first Dominican entered England, and thirteen years before Langton summoned proctors to convocation." Pasquet, another eminent worker in this field, sees no ground for the supposed Dominican influence on de Montfort and the parliament of 1265.

We have examined the problem of the Dominicans and Parliament in terms of its historical environment and in the perspective of recent critical investigations. Something must also be said of important obstacles that still face the source-hunter. It will always be necessary in pursuing this chapter in the history of representation to distinguish clear evidence of contact between the two representative systems from evidence of mere resemblance. Only the first kind can be taken as conclusive proof. Professor Barker's theory of diffusion through the Dominicans to England fails to convince principally because he is too apt to jump to conclusions when he sees

that one institution looks like another and precedes that other in date. He claims, for example, that the calling up by Langton of delegates from the monasteries and lower clergy in 1226 was probably due to the fact that Langton, a patron of the Oxford house, was impressed by Dominican practice. When we know why this convocation was called, the argument is less convincing. Honorius III in that year asked for a supplementing of the papal revenue by regular allocations from the episcopal and monastic revenues, and from each collegiate church. In France and in Germany as well as in England *special assemblies* of the clergy were convened to answer the request. Langton thereupon summons delegates from those monasteries and collegiate churches which, it is proposed, will be taxed for the first time. Do we need any other reason to explain this innovation in procedure?

The source-hunter, then, needs something more than evidence of structural resemblance between the Dominican chapters, convocation, and the King's Council. The case for or against Barker's thesis will not be complete until we know more fully and more accurately the careers of the intermediaries.

# Roman Law and Representation

**GAINES POST**

Gaines Post (1902–    ), Professor of Medieval History at Princeton, published articles in *Speculum* and *Traditio* in 1943 which stressed the importance of Roman and canon law theories in the origins of representation. These articles have been published with other publications of Post in his *Studies in Medieval Legal Thought: Public Law and the State, 1100–1322* (1964). In the selection below, taken from *Traditio* (1943), Post argues that the *plena potestas* (full powers) of parliamentary representatives implied a judicial, procedural consent to royal measures, rather than a political, sovereign consent. At the same time, Post compares parliamentary procedure to that of ordinary courts, raising anew the question, was parliament concerned with judicial or political affairs?

Long before Henry III summoned delegates with full powers to Parliament in 1268, the precedent for his writ was created not only in Romano-canonical court and ambassadorial procedure, but also in the convocation of imperial and papal assemblies in Italy. Delegates (consuls and judges) of Lombard communes had attended the Diet of Roncaglia in 1158; but what their powers were is not clear, except that they were subservient to Frederick Barbarossa. Our formula emerges clearly in 1200: Pope Innocent III summoned to his Curia *responsales* or *procuratores* [legal agents] from six cities; they must have *plenaria potestas* to meet with the pope, to consult (*tractare*), to bring *consilium* on the establishment of law and order in the Papal States, to render the services of *expeditionem, parlamentum, pacem et guerram* [military aid, advice, peace and war] and to accept the papal will in these matters and in the paying of an annual *census*. These proctors, in a feudal *curia* or assembly, obviously came provided with full powers to submit to the pope's orders, not to refuse obedience and limit the papal authority. It is probable that, from 1215 on, proctors sent by cathedral chapters to general and provincial councils and by secular communities to the assemblies of Frederick II or to the Cortes of Aragon and Castille, often had "full powers" or the equivalent. But since the mandates themselves have rarely survived from the first half of the thirteenth century, very few instances of the actual use of *plena potestas,* until the latter half of the century, can be given. Yet *plena potestas* must have enjoyed some popularity because of its legal importance. When the *generalissimum* Chapter of the Dominican Order met at Paris in 1228, it was attended by twelve provincial priors, each of whom was accompanied by two *diffinitores* as "deputies" of the provincial chapter, which had conferred *potestas plenaria* on them. These provincial priors and *diffinitores,* however, were more than ordinary representatives; although they were elected, by the election they became administrators and judges, and as such, in the meeting of the General Chapter they constituted a high council and court rather than a representative assembly.

But other representatives in ecclesiastical assemblies, such as proctors of cathedral chapters and of dioceses, and *socii* [dele-

From Gaines Post, *"Plena Potestas* and Consent in Medieval Assemblies: A Study in Romano-Canonical Procedure and the Rise of Representation, 1150–1325," *Traditio,* I (1943), pp. 368–375, 407–408. Reprinted by permission of Fordham University Press.

gates] elected by the convents to attend provincial chapters of the Dominicans, had the powers of ordinary proctors for litigating, negotiating, petitioning, carrying the record and information, and accepting the decisions of bishops or of priors and *diffinitores*. These powers at first were not usually stated as *plena potestas;* but they were practically the same as the general and special mandates given by communities with the usual clause of *ratihabitio* [clause in which the person represented promised to ratify the actions of his delegate] along with the instructions.

After the middle of the thirteenth century the use of *plena potestas* was frequent. By 1300, it was normal to use it in sending representatives to assemblies, whether provincial councils, chapters of the religious (monks and friars), general councils, or high courts and councils of princes (to the English Parliament by 1268, or possibly earlier; to the Cortes of Aragon by 1307, and probably much earlier; and to the French States General in 1302 and thereafter.)

*Plena potestas* in ordinary judicial procedure signified the litigants' full acceptance of, or consent to, the court's decision of the case. However slow this procedure was because of the numerous excuses and delays granted to the litigants, the theory of judicial consent recognized the superior jurisdiction of the court. But, of course, the power, or *imperium,* of the court depended not only on legal definitions but also on the actual power of the government which claimed the right to enforce the law of the land. Thus in a well-centralized State, under a strong monarch, the royal courts had sufficient jurisdiction to enforce legal procedure, to summon accused parties, to enforce consent by inflicting penalties for contumacy or default, to interpret the powers given the agents of parties, to pass sentence, and to grant or refuse the right of appeal. These rights of jurisdiction were limited by the slowness of the procedure which was developed to guarantee due process as a protection of all private rights

brought into litigation. Nevertheless, if private rights were protected by the principles of law and justice and by the theory that every legal right was accompanied by the right of consent to any change affecting it, the courts enjoyed the superior right of interpreting the legality of private rights and the quality of private consent. Judicial, procedural consent, that is consent to the decision of the court, was obviously not voluntary — it was no limitation of the *imperium* of the king and his judges. The king's judicial power in this respect was limited not by the *plena potestas* of representatives in his courts but by the law of the land according to which he must judge.

Did *plena potestas,* however, mean the same kind of consent in a royal assembly? The procedure by which representatives were summoned and by which they brought powers from corporate communities, defended the "liberties" of their constituencies, and accepted the will of king and council was quite analogous to that of litigation in courts ordinary. But the assembly was no ordinary court: the king was the highest judge and administrator in the land; he presided over the assembly in the fullness of his prerogative; and the essential core of the assembly was the king's high court and council before which magnates and delegates appeared in assembly. More important, representatives were not summoned to the assembly as litigant parties in the ordinary sense; they were summoned primarily to consent to an extraordinary demand by the king for a subsidy. Thus, even if the royal assembly be looked upon as a high court, analogy alone will not explain the *plena potestas* of representatives; for the whole institution of national representation was extraordinary, even though it developed logically out of ordinary Romano-canonical court procedure as adapted to the feudal *curia* as high court, council, and assembly. Judicial procedure, therefore, is by itself insufficient to explain the formula. Any conclusive interpretation must depend on a careful estimate of the royal prerogative in the face of individual and community rights recognized by law and custom.

When the king of England, for example, needed an extraordinary subsidy, feudal law demanded that he obtain the consent of all whose rights and liberties were affected, and this consent was voluntary — witness Magna Carta, c. 12 and 14. But in the thirteenth century, under the influence particularly of Roman law, the legal experts of popes and kings were beginning to assert the doctrine that an emergency, the case of necessity, which was usually the just war of defense against an invader, touched both king and kingdom, the *status regis et regni*, the rights and welfare of the people — and not only the rights of tenants-in-chief, but also the relatively new rights of lesser free men in the communities of shires and towns, which were not, strictly speaking, a part of the feudal system, but which by the very attainment of a jurisdictional status and of certain liberties granted by the king were now directly touched by the national emergency. Therefore, partly under the influence of the principle that what touches all must be approved by all, it was becoming necessary for both feudal magnates, who no longer fully represented others' specific rights except in certain feudal customs, and knights and townsmen to consent to measures which must inevitably cause some sacrifice of all liberties guaranteed by custom and law. To meet the emergency or danger, the king, who represented the kingdom, must for the common utility and public safety raise an adequate army. For this he needed more money than feudal custom gave him, and consequently, for the common good he had a superior right to ask his subjects for an aid. Indeed, his prerogative "meant that reserve of undefined power necessary to any government to enable it to deal with emergencies" which affected the *status* of the king and the whole community of the realm. It was the king's right to deal with the emergency: for the common good he claimed a superior jurisdiction in order to suppress disturbers of the peace within the kingdom, made a new law for a new situation with the counsel and consent of his council, and of all whom the matter touched. Similarly, with the common counsel and consent of all, he levied an extraordinary subsidy for the defense of all who had rights (that is, the king and the whole community of individuals and communities) in the case of necessity — which was usually a war. Much of this theory, which already in the thirteenth century reflected a dawning conception of public right and state sovereignty as a means of defeating private or feudal rights, was derived from the Roman law.

When a state of emergency existed (and it was the king and his council who had the right to declare the case of necessity, although they still must persuade the assembly that there was no pretext in the declaration), the king, by his general prerogative as well as by his more specific powers of administration and jurisdiction, had the right to demand aid in order to meet the danger which touched the welfare of all — *status regis* and *status regni*. He therefore had the right to summon all to grant him the resources for defending *l'estat du roialme*. If by the law the community had the right to be summoned (the king could do nothing of a really extraordinary nature without consulting the interested parties), nonetheless the right and power of summoning in these circumstances were greater than the privilege of being summoned. The king's ordinary jurisdiction and administrative authority lay in the background; but his prerogative enhanced his power to summon and to punish for contumacy. He must summon, but those summoned must respond or suffer by default.

Perhaps, then, the analogy is not so farfetched as one might suppose: even in public matters that were not of the nature of private affairs tried in court, the assembly of the whole community met before (*coram* is the usual word) the king and his council; rather, it met before the king in his court in his council. The king presided over the assembly, not as a mere president or chairman but as the highest administrator, judge, and legislator representing the public good. He and his council, before summoning representatives, decided that an emergency existed and that the whole community should help meet the danger common to all. The representatives were needed by the government to report how much their constituents could give by way of a subsidy; their constituents were interested in appointing representatives in order that their rights might be protected and that they might protest against a too burdensome tax. When it was almost a foregone conclusion that they would have to grant a subsidy, the communities might want to delay or to refuse to send delegates. But in an emergency the royal government needed the money at once and could tolerate neither delay nor refusal. Having a superior right to demand a subsidy, the king, following ordinary judicial procedure, demanded that the communities give their representatives *plena potestas,* that is, such full powers that quick action and legal consent would result. *Plena potestas,* therefore, was to an assembly what it was to a court: it was in theory an expression of consent, given before the action, to the decision of the court and council of the king. The case of necessity was, as it were, tried in the assembly, and the representatives were, in a sense, attorneys protecting the rights and interests of the communities against the royal claim of public utility and binding the communities by their consent to the decision.

In another sense the king, too, was a defendant — insofar as he had to prove the case of necessity and his honest intent to act for the public and common welfare. Yet he was no more a defendant than a modern State which, while granting a hearing to all whose property rights are touched, compels men to sell land for a public highway or an artificial lake — the right of eminent domain for the public good is superior to private rights. And, as said above, it was relatively easy for the king and his government to make good their case. Nevertheless, the representatives could defend local and private interests by presenting petitions containing grievances, by negotiating on the amount of the subsidy demanded, by arguing against the need of a subsidy, and by trying to obtain promises of no-precedent. In turn, the king and council had the power to hear and to grant or deny the petitions, although generally promises were made to remedy the grievances presented. After such hearings and minor decisions, the king's court and council announced the decision as to the amount of the subsidy, and the assembly formally consented to the will of the government — unless, as it rarely happened, the king had been forced to withdraw his demand because of being unable to prove that a "national" emergency, such as the danger of invasion, really existed. Consent even to taxation was therefore consultative and judicial, not voluntary and democratic. Only when Parliament ceased to be a council and court, in effect, and when the king was deprived of the practical right to refuse a common petition, could *plena potestas* signify in England popular sovereignty. . . .

The practical application of [*plena potestas*] in the assemblies, the manner in which the representatives carried out their powers, their organization and methods of agreeing among themselves on a common policy or response to the demands made of them, and the particular circumstances which an able opportunism could shape into a defeat for the government — these are a few of many problems that need further investigation if we are to understand how the practice sometimes departed from the theory: how, for example, full powers implied, at least on occasion, a more effective consent in Aragon than in England. Yet the legal theory — if properly kept in relationship with the general legal and political ideas of the time; if properly viewed against the background of feudal law and custom, individual and community rights or liberties hierarchized like medieval society itself, royal and papal authority, and the renewed conception of the superior right of State for the public utility; and if properly considered as capable of interpretation by the judges in royal and papal courts — is an indispensable aspect of representative institutions, whether it was cause, accompaniment, or result of the rise of representation, or all three at the same time.

An essential part of the legal environment was the revival of Roman law and the development of Romano-canonical procedure, which helped corporate and quasi-corporate communities become bearers of individual rights of lesser free men and stimulated the application of the procedure of representation in such a manner that local interests could be defended and obligations to the government fulfilled. Of all the terminology taken from the Roman law and accepted throughout western Europe by the middle of the thirteenth century, *plena potestas* was one of the most significant expressions of the new relationship between the communities and the central authority. It meant the acceptance of the right and power of the ruler to summon, ask for information, and demand consent to measures decided for the common good and safety. It meant the right of the communities to be summoned, to elect representatives and instruct them on how to defend local rights, to negotiate for a reasonable subsidy or beneficial statute and to consent to the decisions of the king and his council. Without precluding the right of representatives to oppose the wishes of the government by judicial means, it meant such full instructions and powers of consent that the king's prerogative could not be limited by *referendum*. If the ruler must consult with, and secure the consent of all who were touched by the business by compelling communities to give full powers to their delegates, he bound them to the central authority. *Plena potestas,* then, stood not for political, sovereign consent but for judicial-conciliar consent to the decisions of the prince and his high court and council.

We must therefore neither exaggerate nor underestimate the value of *plena potestas*. It was not, as J. G. Edwards has maintained, one of the roots of the legal sovereignty of Parliament, for it was interpreted by the royal court and was subordinate to the prerogative; it could be such a root only if other forces deprived the king of his actual judicial and administrative powers. Nor was *quod omnes tangit* the second root of popular sovereignty; it was more a principle of judicial process than of political consent. On the other hand, *plena potestas* was no symbol of abject surrender to the will of the monarch. It was used partly because all interested parties had the right to be summoned, for by law and custom the government could do nothing extraordinary without consultation and consent. Even Philip IV of France summoned the third estate and the lower clergy for a better and more compelling reason than the mere desirability of propaganda and publicity: by the legal fictions of the period he could not appeal to a General Council in a case that touched king and kingdom without obtaining the consent of the community of the realm to the act of appeal. Consent was usually forthcoming, especially when the government could present a clear case of necessity and public utility — and exert real pressure. Nonetheless, absolutism was made impossible by the very theory of judicial consent and by the procedure of obtaining that consent through the full powers of representatives. Joined with the prevailing theory of rights and consent to any changes affecting them, *plena potestas* was, in favorable circumstances, a means of defending local liberties and individual rights and an essential part of a system of judicial and conciliar representation based on that law of the land by which the prince must rule.

If it be argued that *plena potestas* and accompanying terms in the documents, such as *quod omnes tangit, status regni,* and *necessitas,* were nothing more than a *flatus vocis,* the answer is that legal terminology then as now was developed by legal experts to withstand challenge in the courts, and that royal and papal judges were guided by the legal language in reaching decisions and in interpreting the law. If it be argued that the terminology was merely a matter of procedure and not of the essence of the law, the answer is that up to a certain point procedure is itself of that essence, for without a well-formulated procedure the benefit of the law is denied. *Plena potestas* was perhaps a legal fiction, but in court, fiction is often more powerful than fact.

# English Local Communities and Representation

## HELEN MAUD CAM

In the selection below, Helen Cam evaluates the significance of recent research into corporate and Roman law theories of the origins of representation; yet she still insists that these continental explanations cannot be made to fit the English experience, which was "absolutely exceptional."

THOUGH REPRESENTATION is an old, not to say hackneyed subject, we can never get away from it. It is the basis of our Anglo-American assumptions about democracy, though unknown to the Greeks who invented the word democracy and repudiated by Rousseau, the prophet of modern democracy. Representative institutions are the background of Stubbs' great book. His design of the growth of the English constitution proceeds from the history of the things represented to that of the series of events by which the principle and practice of representation were incorporated in the national assembly. I use the word *things* (which we are at such pains to eliminate from the undergraduate essay) advisedly, for the problem, as I should like to pose it, is "*What* is represented, and why?"

In the last twenty years the study of this ancient subject has been reinvigorated from two new sources, each of them originating outside England. . . . In 1933, at the International Congress of Historical Sciences held at Warsaw, a Belgian scholar, M. Émile Lousse, . . . propounded to the assembled historians a project for a concerted study of the formation of assemblies of estates. The *Ständestaat,* the *état corporatif* — the realm of estates — had long been a subject of study in Germany; two articles by Otto Hintze, published in the *Historische Zeitschrift* in 1929 and 1931, had set forth the theory that the evolution of estates was the clue to the later medieval history not merely of Germany but of all western Christendom. This view, in tune with the new corporatism which Italy and Germany were translating into fact and which La Tour du Pin had been preaching in France for many years, appeared to the historians at Warsaw worthy of scientific investigation; and in 1935 the international commission for the study of assemblies of estates came into being, with M. Coville as its president and M. Lousse as its secretary and driving force.

From Helen Cam, "The Theory and Practice of Representation in Medieval England," *Law-finders and Law-makers in Medieval England* (Barnes & Noble, Inc., 1963), pp. 159–175. Reprinted by permission of The Merlin Press (London), and of the author.

Conferences were held year after year, mostly under the auspices of the French *Société d'Histoire de Droit;* volumes of studies by French, Swiss, Belgian, Hungarian, Italian and English scholars were published, on various aspects of the history of estates, and the first volume of Professor Lousse's own book on corporative organization and representation came out in occupied Belgium in 1943. It was followed in 1949 by Signor Marongiu's book, *L'istituto parlamentare in Italia dalle origine al 1500,* and [in 1952] by Mr. Richardson's and Professor Sayles' book on *The Irish Parliament in the Middle Ages.* . . .

This digression is not altogether irrelevant. In our study of English medieval history, we are, perhaps, too ready to stay on our island. Considering the very close relations between England and Rome, and England and France during the greater part of the middle ages, our reluctance to look overseas and study parallel developments for enlightenment, is rather less than scientific. If English and American scholars have been roused to protest by some of the statements made about English institutions in the volumes I have mentioned, the result has, I think, been only beneficial; but I have the impression that considerably more attention has been paid to them in the United States than in England. The outcome should be, I think, first, a stimulus to the use of the comparative method; secondly, a re-examination of our own views. It is attack that compels one to define and justify assumptions that may never have been formulated.

Some of Professor Lousse's criticisms in detail can be answered fairly readily. He does very much less than justice to Stubbs, whose learning stands on a rock, however much his interpretations may be affected by the ebb and flow of circumstance. M. Lousse went so far as to say that Maitland, "who taught at Cambridge," did not think much of Stubbs (an Oxford professor) and published a course of lectures in opposition to him, where he showed his knowledge of western Christendom (in opposi-

tion to Stubbs' insularity), by referring to the idea of the three estates of those who pray, those who fight and those who work. The fact is that Maitland expressly referred his Cambridge students to Stubbs' fifteenth chapter, not only for the phrase he quotes but also for a fuller discussion of the history of estates in France, Germany, Sicily, Aragon, Castile, Naples, and the Netherlands, than he, Maitland, had time to give.

The conception of estates of the realm is indeed not a new one to American and English students of history, for whom McIlwain's chapter in the seventh volume of the Cambridge Medieval History has amplified Stubbs' sketch. The classification of society into those who pray, those who fight, and those who labour, is a medieval commonplace, to be found in Alfred the Great and Aelfric, in Langland and Wyclif, in Gerson and Nicholas of Clamangis; it is familiar in Germany in the three categories of *Lehrstand, Wehrstand, Nährstand.* Dumézil indeed would say that it goes back to the origins of the Indo-European peoples and is one of their basic social and religious conceptions, being reflected in the three Hindu castes of priests, fighters and cultivators — Brahmani, Kshathiza, Vaisya; in the Druids, warriors and agriculturists of primitive Celtic society, in the three tribes and three deities of primitive Rome — Jupiter, Mars, Quirinus; in the three Scandinavian deities, Odin, Thor and Freya. A cruder but more recent expression of it is in the inn-sign of the Four Alls, on which are depicted side by side, the parson saying "I pray for all"; the soldier saying "I fight for all"; the labourer, "I work for all," and the king, "I rule all."

Such a view of society is functional, vocational; it does not of itself indicate the common consciousness or common action that goes with the idea of estates of the realm, or the *Ständestaat.* There may well be division of function in the lord's household or the king's realm; but so long as the functionaries are the tools of their lord, as

Alfred called them, and so long as the horizontal principle of the associations of like with like has not yet triumphed over the vertical principle of loyalty to and dependence upon the lord, so long society is still in the feudal stage. It is changing economic conditions, what we used to call "the rise of the middle class," that produces the sense of common interest with one's equals, common aims, common action against one's enemies (often one's superiors), and that leads to the formation of associations and the organization of societies by estates. To take one instance: such a stage is reached· when the English bishops begin to regard themselves, and be regarded primarily, as members of the clerical estate, rather than as tenants in chief, owing service at the king's court "like the other barons"—*sicut barones ceteri,* as the Constitutions of Clarendon phrase it. Stubbs notes the corresponding moment in Aragon as occurring in 1301.

For Professor Lousse the process of association is clear cut and deliberate. It follows a regular pattern of mutual oaths — *conjurationes* or *communiones;* of pacts like that of the citizens of London in 1193 or of the community of the baronage of Oxford in 1258. M. Petit-Dutaillis in his last book insisted that it is in this mutual oath that the *sine qua non* of the French commune consists, not in any specific privilege or status. For M. Lousse, however, there is a second stage; the *corporation,* whether urban, mercantile, or noble, that has been constituted by oaths, must secure legal status; it must obtain a charter of privileges from the governmental authority in order to become an estate and not merely a group. A number of corporations may combine to appeal for privileges and thus establish themselves as an order. He has a rich collection both of pacts and of charters of privileges to bear out his contention. But it is here that the formula begins to look foreign to the student of English institutions.

Confronted with the charge of obstinate insularity and national pride, which M. Lousse hurls against him, the English historian examines the tendencies of English social and constitutional evolution to see how they look in the light of the continental formula. Yes, there are gilds; yes, there is at least one sworn commune; yes, there are charters to boroughs, and charters of liberties to the barons, and to the clergy (though the English historian is a little startled to find the Constitutions of Clarendon and the Statute of Mortmain listed among the concessions of liberties to the English church). Yes, there is — but only for a fleeting moment — a *communitas bachelerie*.[1] But the only lasting associations and corporations that we are aware of in England are the gilds and companies, the universities and colleges, and the religious houses and orders. There is no closed or sworn order or fraternity of nobles, and even less of knights; there are no charters to groups of towns. The associations of magnates for the obtaining of privileges are occasional and ephemeral; they are not part of the permanent order of English society. As with Pirenne's formula for the growth of towns, so with M. Lousse's formula for the corporative state; England is the square peg that will not fit into the round hole.

There are two main reasons for this, as it seems to me — the economic and the political — or rather one that combines the two and is even more basic — the chronological. It is the timing in England that differs from that of the continent. Owing to the circumstances of the Norman conquest, which wedded military efficiency to the fairly advanced institutions of the Anglo-Saxon monarchy, England had something like one hundred years' start on France in the evolution of a royal administrative system. Neither the great feudatories who confronted the Capetian dynasty, nor the imperfectly feudalized re-

[1] The "community of bacheors" were, according to Sir F. M. Powicke, members of baronial households who belonged to a knightly class but were not yet knighted. Under pressure from these men in 1259, the barons were forced to accept the Provisions of Westminster. [Editor's note.]

gionalisms of the Empire, were present to impede the growth of Anglo-Norman and Angevin authority; the beginnings of the *Beamtenstaat,* the bureaucracy, which, on the continent, came to be the dominant character of the great monarchies and princedoms of the fourteenth and fifteenth centuries, are traceable in England from the twelfth century onwards.

But if England is administratively and politically ahead of the continent, she is economically behind. She has her commercial and industrial features — we all know about the tribe of foreign merchants in the port of London in the days of Ethelred — but compared with the ferment in the valleys of the Po, the Rhine and the Scheldt, or even in northern France, her urban and industrial developments are on a small scale. Weaker and less institutionalized central authorities on the continent are confronted by denser populations, with more urgent economic problems and more substantial resources, which in their turn, it may well be, stimulate the nobles into a more class-conscious solidarity. The pacts, the corporations, and the orders of the continent are the product of conditions that do not obtain in England.

Nevertheless, this new angle of vision is illuminating, and we need be in no hurry to reject the light it may give us. Certain old commonplaces and recent interests take a fresh colour, for instance, the rise to prominence of the expression *communitas* in the thirteenth century, commented on by Stubbs, Jolliffe and Powicke, among many others. Tait in his book *The Medieval English Borough,* as he relates the appearance of the mayor in the English borough to the wave of communal sentiment coming from France, points out that John, who had sanctioned the commune of London on his brother's behalf in 1191, appealed fourteen years later to the commune of the realm, the *communa liberorum hominum* [community of free men], for the defence of the kingdom against a threatened French invasion in 1205. You will remember how the phrase and possibly the sentiment was turned against John in 1215, when the twenty-five guarantors of Magna Carta were empowered as a last resort to grieve and distrain the king *cum communia totius terrae* [with the community of the entire country]. When, under John's son, the expression *communitas regni* or *communitas terrae* [community of the realm] recurs more and more frequently, it should have for us now overtones evoked by the continental events to which Lousse and Petit-Dutaillis have been calling our attention. The oath taken by the *comune de la tere* at Oxford is absolutely in the continental tradition.

Or again there is the petitionary process, so intimately bound up with the judicial and legislative activities of early parliaments, so fruitfully studied in recent years by H. L. Gray, H. G. Richardson, G. O. Sayles, G. L. Haskins, D. Rayner, and A. R. Myers. This may profitably be examined afresh in relation to the rich material furnished by Lousse in his fourth chapter. We are still very much in the dark as to the genesis of the petitions, whether singular or common, that were presented to the king and his council in the thirteenth and fourteenth centuries. Who drew up the Petition of the Barons of 1258? and how were the *Monstraunces* of 1297 drafted? or the complaints of the rectors of Berkshire in 1240? In the ninth chapter of *Henry III and the Lord Edward,* Powicke has suggested that "the growing coherence of the clergy probably influenced the *communitas* of the barons and made it more conscious"; it seems not improbable that the clerks who drafted the *gravamina* [complaints] of their own order had the lion's share in moulding the petitionary technique, with its immense potentialities for the future.

In M. Lousse's attack on the *parlementarisme* of Stubbs he was not in 1943 aware of the formidable allies he possessed. He ignored all the undermining of the seventeenth- and eighteenth-century conceptions of primitive democratic institutions by the erection in 1893 of the high court of parliament as a royal and judicial elder brother who had ousted the younger brother, the embryonic house of commons, from the place of honour. But Stubbs' picture — not quite as black and white as some allege — has had to face criticism from a third quarter.

In the same year that M. Lousse's book came out, there appeared two important articles by Mr. Gaines Post of the University of Wisconsin on "*Plena Potestas* and Consent" and on "Roman Law and Early Representation in Spain and Italy," in which he demonstrated, with a wealth of learning, how great was the contribution of Roman and Canon Law to the theory and practice of medieval representation. Medieval representation, he says, was constructed of heterogeneous materials on a foundation of feudal law, local institutions, royal curias, ecclesiastical synods, and the growth of royal and papal authority, but in both ideas and procedure its architects were greatly aided by the revival of Roman Law in the eleventh and twelfth centuries. In his articles on *plena potestas* Mr. Gaines Post has convincingly linked the early summoning of representatives to assemblies in Spain and Italy with the Roman lawyers' device of the plenipotentiary attorney representing his principal in a court of law: a conception that fits in very neatly with the *persona ficta* [fictitious person] of M. Lousse's corporations.

In face of all these attacks, are our English knights of the shire and burgesses to retire meekly into the background, saying, as they do to king and lords in 1348, "As to your war and its array, we are so ignorant and simple that we know nothing about it nor can give any counsel in the matter"?

It was a deceptive reply and a pregnant negative; the rolls of parliament show that they took four days of discussion to arrive at it. We also should not be in a hurry to write off the representative element in the English parliaments as irrelevant in the thirteenth and fourteenth centuries. *Sus-*

*tine modicum,* as the senior clerk said to his junior in the exchequer in 1177 when he asked him a tricky question; *Sustine modicum: ruricolae melius hoc norunt —* "Wait a bit; let us ask the country folk."

There are really two issues: What is represented by the representatives? And what is the origin of the device of representation? M. Lousse alleges that it is a corporation or association that is represented, and one recognized if not created by royal charter, Mr. Gaines Post very rightly emphasizes the authoritarian and legalistic aspects of the device as used by twelfth- and thirteenth-century rulers, and, as Stubbs and others have done before him, points out ecclesiastical precedents. But the earliest reference to representation in England occurs in a slightly old-fashioned record of local custom that can be dated soon after 1110, whilst the earliest instance of political representation outside England is in the year 1136, in Italy. There is no need to deny the influence of the Church; it must have been operative in England at any date after A.D. 600. On the other hand, "representation" is a far from unequivocal expression, as is made clear, for instance, in de Lagarde's brilliant analysis of its various significations in the days of Ockham. But long before jurists and scholastics began examining into the bearing of the word, representation, the thing itself, was already on the scene as an obvious common-sense solution of constantly recurrent problems. If you want to get the opinion of a crowd, whether of children or of adults, you will in effect say, "Don't all talk at once — who will speak for you?" If an agreement on action has been arrived at by a group of people, one man will naturally be empowered to act for them. If a job has to be done for which a body of .persons will be held responsible, it is mere common sense for them to arrange among themselves that one or two shall do it and leave the others free to get on with the work of food production, or business, or whatever it may be. These problems, you will note, arise when there is an active community upon which some external demand is made. That is all that is needed to produce some form of representation. The precise nature of the link between community and representative, and between the community and the source of the external demand will be worked out in practice and defined, as becomes necessary, by custom and, in due course, by written law, and last of all, perhaps, in theory.

So we are driven back to our starting point — what is the community that is represented? This is where Stubbs comes into his own and the obstinate insularity of our "nationalist" historians is vindicated. In English sources, the oldest unit to be represented is the vill, in 1110; the next is the shire and hundred, in 1166; the next is the cathedral chapter, in 1226; the next is the diocesan clergy, in 1254; the next is the "community of the land" — otherwise the barons — in 1258; and the next, the borough in 1265.

The representation of the clergy is clearly inspired by canonist doctrine, and can be associated with Innocent III's enunciation of the principle that links representation with consent — *quod omnes tangit ab omnibus approbetur*. In the case of the borough we have a corporation of Lousse's sort; boroughs owe the privileges which make them boroughs to a royal grant; and the practice of summoning representatives of towns to assemblies had precedents in Italy and Spain from 1162 on, representatives who, from 1214 onwards, come as plenipotentiaries with power to bind those who send them, a device which, as Mr. Post has shown, is directly traceable to papal influence.

But with the earlier instances we are in a different world. The vill, the hundred and the shire are not voluntary associations privileged by royal charter, nor is the community of the barons who, at Oxford, have to elect twelve of their number to attend the parliaments that are to meet thrice a year, to treat of common needs and common business with the king's council. (One of the twelve, it should be noted, is a bishop, who on "functional" principles has no business there.) The twelve are to have power to act on behalf of the community of barons; and the purpose of the device is to save the pockets of the barons who cannot afford such frequent journeys to court: *Ceo serra fet pur esparnier le cust del commun* [this is to reduce the cost to the community] — a sound and practical reason.

It is a reason, moreover, that links up with that given in the *Leges Henrici,* in its account of the attendance of the representatives of villagers at the shire and hundred moots. In theory, it implies, all the village might be expected to come; but either the lord of the village or his steward can discharge the obligation of the whole vill; failing that, the reeve, the priest and four of the better men of the vill should attend in place of (*pro*) all the village. Again, a commonsense delegation to one or two of a common responsibility. Whether this was a new practice under Henry I, or a recording of ancient custom, as Stubbs assumed, there is nothing to show; both William the Conqueror and Henry I stressed their preservation of the customs of Edward the Confessor, but we know that they also introduced new practices.

The first reference to representation of the shire, however, does sound like a new practice. In 1166 Henry II provided that if criminals arrested under the new procedure of the jury of indictment could not be brought before a royal justice in their own shire, they should be sent to the nearest royal session in some other shire, and with them, the sheriff was to bring two lawful men of the hundred and township where they had been arrested to bear the record of the shire and the hundred as to why they had been arrested. Neither shire nor hundred court kept a written record of their proceedings; only the oral testimony of "credible men of the court," the ancient "witness of the shire," could be produced to prove what had occurred. And this record, it must be remembered, binds those whom they represent, in the sense that the whole shire may be penalized for the action they report. This is not the same relationship as that of a jury which commits no one beyond itself. Nevertheless, when the jurors give their information to the king's inquisitors in 1086, Domesday Book notes that the "hundred says" so and so, and Stubbs does not seem to be going too far in bringing the jury into his picture of the origins of representation.

We may fully accord to Mr. Edwards the essential importance of the formula of *plena potestas* that rivets the power of the representatives to bind those who send them, we may fully accept Mr. Post's demonstration that that formula is of Roman origin, like the *plene instructi* [fully instructed] of the clerical proctors; but it is clear that the conception in England is older than the adoption of the formula. The burgesses summoned to the council of 1268 had to bring with them letters from their community declaring that they would hold as accepted and established whatever these men should do on their behalf; the community of the barons in 1258 had agreed to hold as established whatever the twelve whom they had elected should do; and men who bore the record of the shire might in fact involve the shire in an amercement if they reported an irregular action of the shire court.

I do not wish to insist on this point; no doubt the barons at Oxford had clerical advisers and colleagues; Bracton, himself a clerk learned in the Roman law, undoubtedly worked with them. But I wish to recur to my point — *what* was represented? — and to insist on the old standing of the communities of shire, hundred and township.

The districts called the shire and the hundred, as they existed in 1166, were not so very ancient, perhaps not more than 200 or 250 years old. But the communities of shire and hundred succeeded to the traditions of the folkmoots; the assemblies in which, as the tenth century hundred

ordinance said, men did justice to each other, and folk right, the law of the people, was declared; the *popularia concilia* [assembly of the people] whose existence, as Stenton reminds us, is attested in the days of Coenwulf of Mercia. The continuity of the twelfth-century shire and hundred courts from those assemblies of the tenth century in which the men of the court had done justice to each other under the presidency of ealdorman or reeve is unbroken down to that thirteenth-century session when the sheriff of Lincolnshire had to give up the attempt to do business and close the court because the country gentlemen went on strike and refused to do their duty as doomsmen. Neither Stubbs' assumption (based on a mangled text) that Henry I was reviving a moribund institution, nor Mr. Jolliffe's that Henry II re-created it, is warranted by any objective evidence. For business, for justice, and for publicity the shire court maintained its vitality, though it may well have been livelier and more active in a county of many small freeholders, like Lincolnshire, than in a county that contained many large liberties, like Dorset.

This is not to deny that the policy of the Norman and Angevin kings helped to keep the shire and hundred alive. They preserved them not merely by edicts that compelled the sheriffs to observe ancient custom, but even more by giving them work to do. Edgar had given the hundreds thief-catching duties; William the Conqueror gave them a concern with homicide by the institution of the *murdrum* fine,[2] besides calling on them for information as to the holding of land, well before 1086. Henry II involved them in the reporting of suspects and Henry III gave them military and police responsibilities, for the keeping of watches and furnishing of armour, and demanded more and more information as to royal rights and private liberties and official misdoing from the

[2] A heavy fine imposed by William the Conqueror upon any Anglo-Saxon hundred in which a Norman was murdered. [Editor's note.]

hundred juries. The shire found itself involved in the extension of royal justice and the enlargement of the scope of royal revenues: invited by John to send delegates to discuss the affairs of the realm with the king; invited by Henry III to send delegates in 1227 to report on the sheriff's observance of Magna Carta and in 1254 on the willingness of the shire to contribute to the expenses of the king's wars in France.

Who, in fact, ran the shire court? From M. Lousse's angle, it was the *petite-noblesse* — *de smale heeren* — *les seigneurs bassains* — *the Kleinadel* — though he visualizes them in isolation, each on his own estate, only taking common action in free knightly associations — *Ritterbunde.* The nearest he can get to a shire is a *"localité rurale — une agglomeration plus ou moins dense."* In the three-fold cord of English traditional institutions, he can distinguish only the royal and feudal, he is not aware of the communal. It is true that, broadly speaking, the thirteenth-century shire is the field of the gentry, the knights, the squirearchy. The magnates have ceased to attend it, probably well before 1259; but, though the knights or gentlemen will undoubtedly take the lead in county doings, they will be working with freemen of ungentle blood, yeomen, *valetti,* who may represent the shire at parliaments if knights are not available. All the freeholders of the shire contribute to the expenses of their representative at a fixed rate. And there are no water-tight class barriers — the burgess may be a squire, the agriculturist may buy a town house, the squire's son may marry a villein's daughter, the same man may represent borough and county by turns. And above all, the locality counts. Devonshire will petition the king to have a Devon-born sheriff; and at Oxford the barons will demand that the sheriffs shall not only be landholders, but residents in the shire they administer. The *pays,* the *patria,* the *country,* as the county was still called in Jane Austen's days, of the country gentlemen is the dominant *motif;* however he may

link up with his fellows in the house of commons as an estate of the realm, it is not an order or estate that he represents, but a locality, and the house of commons, when it finally comes into existence, is not a house of *roturiers,* of the non-noble, but a house of communities, urban and rural.

It is this fact, together with the fluidity of social relations in England, that might lead us to maintain the position that Lousse condemns in Stubbs and in other English historians; to reassert *"le caractère absolument exceptionnel du parlement anglais."* It is the survival of the shire that is unique; and it is the shire that makes the English parliament absolutely exceptional.

And at the lowest level of all, the community of the vill has still in the thirteenth century a perfectly definite place in the national system as a community that bears joint responsibility, that can and does take common action in its own interests, that is still represented, as it was in 1110, by its priest, reeve, and four men, or something very like it, and that is declared, in a royal document of the year 1255, to be entitled to prosecute its plaints in the courts by three or four of its own men — as the later legal theory of corporations would phrase it, "to sue and be sued." The very fact that this legal status was lost in later days strengthens the case for the antiquity of the tradition of responsibility and representation in the oldest and smallest community.

How far are we justified in maintaining that this relationship of the ancient communities to representation and to the king's court is absolutely unique and peculiar to England?

The latest contributor to the history of the estates strongly disputes the claim of uniqueness. Mr. Russell Major in his book on *The Estates-General of 1560,* published in 1951 by the Princeton University Press, argues that many of the differences alleged between English and continental representative assemblies did not in fact exist. In France, as in England, the different orders co-operated. The same local assemblies gave mandates to the representatives of the different orders, who were not organized as three distinct houses in the estates-general until well on in the sixteenth century. The class antagonism so often insisted on was not, he maintains, in existence to any degree sufficient to account for the difference in the ultimate fate of the two nations; "the line between noble and non-noble was so vague as almost to defy definition."

A deputy to the estates-general was usually elected and empowered by all three estates, but even when named by a single order of society, local ties bound him as strongly to the other orders of his community as his class tie bound him to members of his estate from other parts of France . . . he represented a particular region whose privileges and autonomy he was carefully instructed to maintain.

Further, the men elected were very often men of considerable experience in local government; and they were not only instructed but paid by those who sent them to the national assembly.

For Mr. Major the key to the different history of the national representative institutions of France and England lies in the strength, not the weakness of local feeling — the regionalism which prevented effective common action from being taken in a meeting of the estates-general, or even in the estates of the Languedoil, and made the provincial estates, rather than the estates-general, the source of financial supply for the crown. The explanation of the greater effectiveness and ultimate survival of the English parliament as against the fading-out of the continental estates is to be found, he maintains, in the policy of the monarchy. Everything turned on the question whether a national representative assembly was or was not of use to the king: if it was, he convoked it; if not, he used the provincial estates in France, the provincial *cortes* in Spain. Mr. Major, whether or not we accept the validity of his arguments, drives us back to look at our facts and our arguments once more, and to ask the question, "What is represented and why?" with renewed determination.

Mr. Chrimes, following on the heels of Maude Clarke, has collected instances to show the emergence of the *term*, "estates of the realm" in England in the fourteenth and fifteenth centuries. It is most conspicuous in connection with the depositions of kings — Edward II, Richard II, Edward V. On the occasions when the king's parliament cannot function, the ingredients that go to make a parliament without a king combine to constitute something like a Convention Parliament of the seventeenth century. The lawyers, like Thirning in 1399, see that, legally speaking, a parliament needs a king. The politicians, like the prior of Canterbury in 1326, see that it is desirable to spread the responsibility for revolution as widely as possible, and to involve in the act of changing the succession as many of the elements of society as can be brought in. Preachers will produce texts and similes to underline the conception of a hierarchical order of society; it is a commonplace; but the estates, though they may be a way of thinking, do not seem to be really of outstanding practical significance. Nor can we get away from the fact that the practice of representation does not apply to the two higher estates. However much the church contributed to the prevalence of the canonist theory, the position of the clergy in parliament does not conform to it. The bishops and abbots are not elected representatives of the clerical order; the diocesan clergy are not in parliament but in convocation. The lay peers of England are not elected by their fellows, they are summoned by the king.

It looks, then, as if we must go back to our traditional formulas, though modified by examination and comparison into something rather different from the Stubbsian pattern. Parliament is both "an assembly of estates and a concentration of local communities," but we couple with this formula the phrase that comes from across the Atlantic: "self-government at the king's command." It was the effective centralization of power under the Angevins that made possible the preservation and utilization of local institutions and local sentiment by the monarchy, which in its turn made possible the growth of the conception of the community of the realm, to which Stubbs directed our attention, and on which Sir Maurice Powicke has so recently insisted. The episode of the villagers of Great Peatling, which Mr. Richardson dug out of the plea rolls for us, with its many-sided social, legal and political implications, may be cited once more in this connection. In 1265 the villagers of this small Leicestershire township could act as a body to meet an emergency; they could, as a community, enter into a contract and be penalized for breaking it; they could sue and be sued, not only by the magnate whose followers they had mishandled, but by individuals of the community itself, and pay damages to them. But Sir Maurice Powicke links up this local episode with political thought on a national scale when he quotes from the record the words by which the men of Peatling Magna justified their attack on the men of a royalist magnate. It was because "they were against the barons and the welfare of the community of the realm" — *contra utilitatem communitatis regni et contra barones*. The fact that in 1265 peasants could speak like this — that the community of the vill was aware of the community of the realm — gives us in a nutshell the clue to the history of representation in England. From such a beginning there could develop what, by Tudor times, was a political commonplace — the conception that all England was represented in the house of commons. A man was there not only for his own locality but for something much more; he was "a publick, a Councellor to the whole State." Though, as Burke was to say long after, the local units were but "inns and resting places," national consciousness had been bred in the *"patria,"* the country, the neighbourhood, and it was there that the foundations were laid which preserved the institutions of representation unbrokenly in the countries of Anglo-Saxon tradition when they perished elsewhere.

# Representation as a European Tradition

## ALEC REGINALD MYERS

Alec Reginald Myers (1912– ), Professor of Medieval History at the University of Liverpool, has written *England in the Late Middle Ages* (1952), "The Character of Richard III" (1954), and "Parliaments in Europe: The Representative Tradition" (1955). He has edited *The Household of Edward IV: The Black Book and the Ordinance of 1478* (1959), and is currently preparing a volume of documents for the period 1327–1485 in the series, *English Historical Documents*, by D. C. Douglas. In the selection below, taken from "Parliaments in Europe," Myers describes early representative assemblies as a Western European, rather than a purely English phenomenon. They were responsible, in part, for the European tradition of limited government.

WHAT ARE the distinctive characteristics of Western democracies? This pressing question of our time cannot be answered without some consideration of their traditions, and the sources of their representative institutions. And as soon as we begin to examine the origins of modern parliamentary government in the western world, we are at once met by what seems to be a direct antithesis between parliamentary history in England and on the Continent. In England, the marks of nearly seven centuries of continuous development of parliament are still both numerous and prominent in our pattern of government. On the Continent, however, it is difficult to trace the stream of modern representative institutions, with their emphasis on popular sovereignty, equality, and the rights of man, farther back than the French Revolution; and it is significant that many people on the Continent prefer to look to that Revolution as the source of modern parliamentary government, regarding with strong disapproval the previous *ancien régime*.

In Britain the sense of the very unusual history of the British Parliament has combined with the trait of insularity to produce a certain indifference to the anteced-ents of parliaments in other Western countries. Even in so great and classic a work as Bishop Stubbs's *Constitutional History of England*, which is essentially a history of the development of the English Parliament to 1485, the representative institutions of contemporary Europe come into the picture in less than 20 pages out of a total of nearly 2,000. This is particularly remarkable when one recalls his wide knowledge of European history and his awareness of its importance. It is true that the general effect of all the immense amount of work that has been done on representative institutions since Stubbs's day has been to vindicate his fundamental standpoint of the unique history, in some decisive respects, of the English Parliament. Professor Helen Cam has lucidly summed this up; in commenting on the theory of the corporative state enunciated by M. Émile Lousse and others, as a formula to explain the growth of representative institutions in Europe, England included, she wrote: "England is the square peg that will not fit into the round hole." Nevertheless, this British tendency towards the isolated study of the English Parliament has important drawbacks; it prevents the illumination of the subject

From A. R. Myers, "Parliaments in Europe: The Representative Tradition," *History Today*, V (1955), pp. 383–390, 446–454. Reprinted by permission of *History Today* and of the author.

by the comparative method, and it leaves undisturbed serious misconceptions as to wherein the uniqueness of English parliamentary history lies.

Thus, it often seems to be assumed in Britain that representative assemblies on the Continent of Europe before the French Revolution were rare, transient, narrow in basis, and weak in power, whereas in fact all these suppositions are untrue. So far from representative assemblies being rare in Europe before 1789, they flourished at one time or another in every state of Latin Christendom. They first emerge clearly towards the end of the twelfth century in the Spanish kingdom of Leon, in the thirteenth century in Catalonia, Sicily, Languedoc, Castile, Portugal, Germany (i.e., the Reichstag), Aragon, Navarre, Bohemia, Brandenburg, Austria, Valencia, Piedmont, England and Ireland; in the fourteenth century in France (i.e., the States-General), the Netherlands, Bavaria, Brittany, Scotland, Normandy, Saxony, Hungary; and in the fifteenth century in Sweden, Denmark, Norway, and Poland. As to the duration of these representative institutions, though some of them disappeared in the seventeenth and the early eighteenth centuries (e.g., in most of the French provinces, Portugal, Naples, some of the German states, Denmark and Norway), in many cases they survived down to the French Revolution.

Another common conception in England about these older parliaments of Europe is that they were very narrow in basis, vigorously defending the exclusive privileges of dominant minorities, and that this was one of the reasons why, on the whole, and in contrast to the English Parliament, they eventually foundered. There is an element of truth in this; but two points should be remembered. One is that before the Victorian age the English Parliament itself rested, by twentieth-century standards, on a narrow basis. When in the Army Council in 1647 Colonel Rainborough put forward the then extremist and fantastic idea of universal suffrage, Cromwell voiced the general reaction, parliamentarian as well as royalist, in his indignant retort: "Where is there any bound or limit set if you take away this limit, that men that have no interest but the interest of breathing shall have no voice in elections?" The other point is that in their period of greatest virility — say, roughly, the fourteenth and fifteenth centuries — these older European parliaments were commonly conceived to represent the whole population of the state, and did in fact normally embrace all the elements that then mattered in politics. In some states — in Sweden, Norway, Denmark, and the Tyrol — the parliament (to give a common name to the Riksdag, Rigsdag, or Landtag) even included, by the end of the fifteenth century, a chamber of peasants; and though this was unusual, it was not uncommon for the election of the deputies of the towns to extend to the immediately surrounding countryside, so that rural communities were not altogether excluded. Moreover, in the intensely aristocratic society of the fourteenth century, juridical theory ordinarily conceived of the nobles as representing, in their capacity as territorial lords, the whole population of what was still a predominantly agrarian society (except in parts of the Low Countries and Northern Italy) — apart from those privileged orders who were represented separately, such as the clergy and the chartered towns. And whatever the form in which the parliament was organized, the nobility were nearly always an essential element.

The commonest arrangement in the fourteenth and fifteenth centuries was a division into three houses or chambers, usually of clergy, nobles and towns — as in Catalonia, Valencia, Portugal, Navarre, the French States-General and most French Provincial Estates, Sicily, the Netherlands, and many German Landtage. Sometimes, however, the parliament sat in two chambers. This might result from the conjunction of the dominant classes to form an upper house (*grand corps*) and of the commoners to form a lower house (*second corps*), as in some French Provincial Estates, or from the fusion of prelates and high officials into a Senate and of elected representatives of nobility and towns to form a Chamber of Deputies, as in Poland and Hungary, or from the disappearance of the clergy at the Reformation, as in the Dutch Netherlands and many of the German Protestant states. In some parliaments, all orders usually sat together in one chamber, although sometimes voting by estates, as in Scotland, Languedoc, and Naples; and by the sixteenth century some parliaments, such as those of Castile and Flanders, were reduced to one estate. This was because the nobles and clergy had gone and only the towns were left; but such a narrow basis for a parliament was rare.

To come now to the last of the four most common misconceptions in England about the character of European representative institutions, it is not true to think of these parliaments as mainly weak and ineffective. It is especially false to think of the English Parliament as always unique, before the French Revolution, in its power over the purse, and in its participation in legislation and justice. On the contrary, the most constant and important activity of these older parliaments in Europe was the granting of taxes. Almost everywhere in Latin Christendom (except Denmark and Norway) the principle was, at one time or another, accepted by the rulers that, apart from the hereditary revenues of the prince, no taxes could be imposed without the consent of parliaments. The German saying that *Landtage sind Geldtage* — representative assemblies are financial assemblies — might well have been applied to nearly all these older parliaments. And on the rock of financial control not only the English Parliament, but many Continental ones, built an imposing edifice of power. It is true that the States-General of France lost this control from the middle of the fifteenth century onwards; but in Britain this has often been taken as more typical of Continental practice than it was, because many British parliamentary historians

have scarcely looked for comparisons beyond France and Castile. The fact is that the States-General of France was, in this respect, exceptional, and that in most countries the exclusive right of the assemblies of estates to grant taxes was, on the whole, well guarded down to the seventeenth century.

If the most constant activity of these older parliaments was the granting — or withholding — of taxes, they were scarcely less active in the field of legislation. All these assemblies claimed the right to present petitions and grievances. It is true that the French States-General and the Castilian Cortes scarcely advanced beyond this, save in times of upheaval and rebellion, and their petitions normally furnished only the stimulus and the basis for the law-making which was still in the hands of the crown. But it is wrong to assume that the English Parliament was the only one that found out how to win effective legislative authority by making grants of supply depend on redress of grievances; nor was the English Parliament the only assembly to try to ensure that the enactments should correspond exactly to their wishes by drawing up their demands in the form of bills ready to become acts as soon as they received the royal sanction. In fact, both these methods came to be practised in many Continental assemblies; in Aragon, Catalonia, Valencia, Sicily, many of the German principalities, Sweden, Poland, Bohemia, and Hungary. The crown usually retained the right to do a certain amount of law-making, in one form or another, without the sanction of parliament; but in general the idea became widespread that parliamentary approval ought to be obtained for all the more important laws. Indeed, in fourteenth- and fifteenth-century Aragon the consent of the Cortes was not only essential for the passing of all laws, but each parliamentary session closed with a formal meeting of king and estates in which all the measures of the session were solemnly proclaimed. This prevented the king from ignoring those doings of the assembly that he did not like. Moreover, a committee of the estates (*Diputación del Reyno*), usually composed of two members of each of the four estates (i.e., of the clergy, the magnates, the *caballeros* or lesser nobility, and the towns), was chosen to remain in existence during intervals between sessions of the Cortes, to watch over the observance of the laws and report to the Cortes any infraction of them. And the Cortes of Aragon, like the parliaments of Poland and many of the German states, also possessed a function which, it is sometimes assumed, belonged to the English Parliament alone: it combined with the functions of a legislative and tax-granting body those of a high court of justice, investigating wrongs done by the king, his officers, or the estates, to one another, to individuals or groups of individuals, of whatever rank, in defiance of the laws, and had the right of demanding that justice should be done.

Finally, we should note that the powers of most parliaments were not entirely limited to tax-granting, legislation and justice. There was a great range of functions claimed by many parliaments, especially in times of confusion and weak government. Most parliaments asserted their views on the conduct of foreign relations. They wanted to have a say in matters of war, peace, treaties and alliances. They often insisted on their right to appoint a regent for an infant prince, to fix the succession to the throne, to stipulate the terms on which each new ruler should be acknowledged on his accession, or even, as in Pomerania and Aragon, to choose a new master if ever the ruler should break his promises or wrong his subjects. The history of most parliaments shows attempts to control the choice of the prince's advisers and ministers and to force upon him a council nominated in parliament. Still more usual was the custom that parliaments should prescribe how the taxes they granted should be spent, or should even undertake this collection and expenditure themselves through their own agents and treasury. In some states, as, for example, Valencia and Cleves, the assembly of estates even claimed and exercised the right to meet for various purposes without a summons from the ruler.

Perhaps this brief survey of the chief functions of these older parliaments of Europe will have served to dispel any notion that they were rare, transient, narrow in basis or weak in power. And if we see that, in one phase of European development, these older parliaments were almost universal throughout Latin Christendom and commonly powerful in their functions, the question naturally arises why this should have happened. Is the explanation simply that this is a stage through which all civilizations pass? This is a problem which has so far not attracted much attention in Britain: but it has aroused the interest of various German historians, especially Otto Hintze and Dietrich Gerhard.

These historians have demonstrated that before the spread of European influence over the rest of the world in the eighteenth and nineteenth centuries, the representative institutions of Latin Christendom were unique. There was no parallel in the absolute monarchies or the city states of the ancient civilizations of the Mediterranean or the Near East. The Aryan invaders of India had a priesthood, a warrior aristocracy, and a peasantry, like the societies of early European civilization; but in the caste-system that subsequently developed in India there was no soil to encourage the growth of representative institutions. There was no room, either, for such a growth in the old China of the fatherly divine authority of the emperor, the bureaucracy of the mandarins, the importance of the family groups, and of conservative custom. Muslim civilization and Japanese culture passed through a phase not unlike that of European feudalism, so that some scholars have used the terms "Islamic feudalism," "Japanese feudalism." But whereas in Europe feudal society was followed by the flowering of assemblies of estates, nothing of the kind seems to have happened in Islam or in Japan. And striking as this difference is, between the culture of Latin Christendom and other civilizations, it is even more remarkable that representative institutions, as Latin Christendom knew them, never developed in Russia. It is remarkable because Russian civilization looked back to Graeco-Roman and Hebrew roots as did that of the West; and if there is the theme of divergence from the West in Russian history, there is also the theme of connexion with it.

It is true that there occurred in sixteenth- and seventeenth-century Russia a number of meetings of an assembly, the *Zemski Sobor*, "The Council of all the land," in which from the beginning of the seventeenth century onwards there were representative elements drawn from the various ranks of society in Moscow and the provinces. But as the Russian historian Kluchevsky has remarked, the *Zemski Sobor* never constituted a political force, but only an administrative aid. It was called into existence by Ivan the Terrible to consider only such questions as he chose to put to it. It owed its transient importance in the early seventeenth century to the temporary need of a Tsar-less land to emerge from anarchy and disorder, and of a new government to strengthen its foothold in the state. The Council was extremely variable in composition; it never evolved any fixed procedure; its competence was never defined; and its decisions were not obligatory on the sovereign in any way whatsoever. . . .

What a different atmosphere is this from that of neighbouring Poland, where from 1652 onwards was being practised in the *Sejm*, or parliament, the famous *liberum veto*, whereby a single member of the *Sejm* could not only thwart the proposal to which he objected but also dissolve the *Sejm* at once! This Russian conception of the relationship between ruler and representative institution is in quite another category from that of fourteenth- and fifteenth-century Aragon, where on the accession of each ruler he was forced to swear to respect all the laws of Aragon and all the rights of the Cortes, and further told that he would continue to be recognized as rightful king if he faithfully executed all the laws that the Cortes should in future make: "and if not, not." (*y si no, no.*)

If, then, in its numerous representative institutions the countries of Latin Christendom had created something unique to Western civilization, we are driven to ask why this should have been so. . . .

Representative institutions in modern Europe and America are often found in conjunction with a republican form of government. But they arose in thirteenth- and fourteenth-century Europe in monarchies, where the prince, representing the unity of the state, and the estates, or *Stände*, representing the manifold interests within the state, stood over against each other, yet necessarily bound together in one organic body. This duality is a fundamental feature of the states of fourteenth- and fifteenth-century Europe, each side having its rights that the other must respect, neither having the right to control the whole life of the state to the exclusion of the other. If, then, it was ordinarily fundamental to this kind of state — the *Ständestaat*, as the Germans have succinctly called it — to have a prince (the Swiss Confederation and North Italian towns were exceptional), a prince who had certain rights but was bound to respect the rights and privileges of others, we have to ask how such a conception of monarchy came to be.

In the beginnings of the history of Western Europe we find one root of this conception in the strong notion among the Germanic peoples that the king was not an absolute lord, able to do as he pleased with his subjects, but the guardian of custom, and that fealty was binding upon the subject only so long as the king also fulfilled his duty. It is true that this notion was not unique to the early Germanic peoples, as some historians have supposed. It is also true that there was in early Germanic kingship another element, pointing towards a very different development — the notion that the king ought to be of the right kin, and that correct blood-relationship to his predecessors, and the correct ceremony of initiation, endowed him with an almost magical efficacy and power. But in the formative centuries of Europe, with their wild disorder and weak government, conditions did not favour the strengthening of the second element, whereas they fostered the development of the first. In Frankia the growth of hereditary kingship was stunted by the displacement of the Merovingian dynasty, which had the sanctity of the right kin-group, by the Carolingian kings, devoid of any hereditary claims, and therefore driven to stress the rightfulness of their rule and their rôle as guardians of law, order and the Church. Though the Church could, and did, exalt the royal authority by the ceremonies of anointing and coronation, which gave the king a quasi-sacred character, and taught that he was God's deputy to whom obedience was due as to one appointed by God, there was a price to be paid. Since the time of St. Augustine of Hippo, there had emerged in the Latin Church a distinctively legal, rational, defining tendency of thought — a tendency sufficiently pronounced and distinctive to arouse later the opposition of the Greek Church. This trend had bred the idea that the divine authority of kingship did not mean irresponsible power; on the contrary, it meant that kingly rule was valid only so long as it was exercised in accordance with divine and natural law, of which the Church was the interpreter. And when, in the eleventh century, the militant Gregorian movement developed in the Church, this view of monarchy came to the fore as an influential force in practical politics — justifying the coercion, deposition, or even the death of a monarch whom the Church should deem to have flagrantly defied the laws by which he had been set on the throne. By comparison with the contemporary Byzantine empire, the princes were weak (save in exceptional cases such as England and Sicily), with only a

rudimentary administration at their disposal, and were further weakened by the rivalries of the manifold states of Europe; whereas the Church was comparatively independent, its strength increased by its character as a European-wide organization and its growing centralized administration.

This tendency of the Latin Church to stress the subjection of the ruler to law was reinforced by another powerful force of the eleventh and twelfth centuries — that of feudalism. In this attempt to restore some stability and order to societies almost shattered into anarchy by the tumults of the ninth century, elements from both the Germanic and the Roman heritage were fused and sharpened into a conception of the mutual rights and obligations of lord and vassal, each having his rights and duties within a framework of feudal law and custom. As Matthew Paris was later to put it: *sicut subditus domino, ita dominus subdito tenetur.* If the lord should disregard his vassal's rights, then the vassal should have the right of resistance; and in a situation where the military power of a ruler depended, not on a subservient, paid army controlled by a docile bureaucracy, but on a feudal host led by a warrior aristocracy as proud, and collectively as strong, as the monarchy, such a conception of the vassal's rights was a potent one. Where feudalism had struck deep, we often find churchmen combining with feudal vassals to recall the ruler to the remembrance (as they saw it) of his subjection to law, and to his duty of ruling with the advice of his great men, clerical and lay. Where feudalism was weak or non-existent, as in Scandinavia, Poland, or Hungary, we find churchmen combining with the warrior aristocracy whose power was based not on fiefs but on the leadership of older kindred and local groupings.

But now we have to remember another factor — the freedom of Western Europe after A.D. 1000 from invasion and conquest from without, except on its margins, as in Poland, Hungary, Austria, and the Adriatic coast. Here is a striking contrast to the fate of Russia, whose history was profoundly affected by the fact that for over 200 years it was struggling to free itself from the Mongolian domination of the Tartars. The greater peace and cohesion now possible in Western Europe meant a more fertile soil for the growth once more of royal authority; it meant, also, favourable conditions for a renaissance that provided the technical devices, especially in finance, for fostering more efficient administration, and also a revival of Roman law, which could furnish powerful doctrines for the enhancement of royal authority. But this very tendency to centralization, and the growth of royal power, itself stimulated a limitation in two ways. In the first place, an expanding administration needed greater resources, and stronger governments, with better weapons at their disposal, led, in a culture of separate and rival states, to an era of longer and more expensive wars. This pressing need for greater income came too quickly for princes to have overcome older notions of the rights of subjects, or at any rate of prelates and magnates, to consent or refuse an imposition on their financial resources; and so, in the circumstances, the needs of the princes could only be met by summoning assemblies of their politically powerful subjects, or representatives of those powerful subjects who were too numerous to come as individuals, in order to ask them for grants of taxation to help the prince in his need.

Secondly, the pressure of the expanding monarchies alarmed those groups that were especially powerful into drawing together into associations for self-defence. As a whole there was no practical alternative to organization for group defence; for, in thirteenth-century Western Europe, threatened groups could not escape the pressure by wholesale emigration. It is true that, as is now more clearly understood, there was considerable internal colonization, or intensification of settlement, in various parts of Western Europe, and there occurred about this time the famous German expansion beyond the Elbe. But these developments, important as they were, did not assume a big enough scale to enfeeble the urge towards the kind of defensive association that spread throughout Latin Christendom. Here is another factor differentiating the history of Western Europe from that of Russia, with its expanding eastern frontier . . . Though Russian history can show us the rough-and-ready, free, self-governing frontier-society of the Cossacks, it also presents to our inquiry a nobility more mobile than that of the West, never forming provincial or local institutions strong enough to resist the government for long or capable of imparting vitality to a representative assembly. The Russian nobility never developed a strong sense of corporate loyalty or group rights. . . . [But] in Western Europe part of the effective core of assemblies of estates was almost everywhere formed by a self-armed warrior aristocracy, as conscious of its rights and its honour as of its duty and its fealty. . . .

The idea of groups privileged in law goes back to the beginnings of Europe, to the exceptional position of the imperial states in the Roman Empire. The idea of laws relating to only a section of the population was strengthened by the operation of separate systems of law for Germanic conquerors and Roman subjects in barbarian successor-states. The notion was assisted by the fact that the Latin Church had lost the protection of a strong government, such as that of the Roman Emperors, and was anxious for the safety and independence of its clergy in a violent and anarchical age; the Church therefore had both the opportunity and the need to insist on a juridically privileged position in society for the clergy. The conception of privilege was further extended by the pressure of a feudal aristocracy, well aware of its usefulness to the prince, conscious of the increasing definition of its duties in customary law, and determined to have its rights also well defined in law. And if the eleventh- and twelfth-century renaissance produced a revival of Roman law, which could be used to strengthen the power of the monarchy, it also led to a great consolidation of canon law, fortifying the legal privileges of the Church and of the clergy. There took place a large extension of the powers of Church courts, controlled by the clergy, exercising important jurisdiction not only over the clergy but over the laity as well; and with the rapid development of centralization in the Church there came the growth of activity and influence throughout Western Europe of the highest ecclesiastical court and immunity of all — the Papal Curia. The piety of the eleventh, twelfth and thirteenth centuries resulted in a great endowment of bishoprics, cathedrals and monasteries, and also in a shower of charters of immunities and privileges from the princes to the bishops of the sees, the deans and chapters of the cathedrals, the abbots and monks of the monasteries.

Moreover, conditions were favourable to the growth of new associations of free men; for not only was there greater peace and order, but the restrictive influence of the kin group on free association had almost entirely disappeared in Western Europe, and the formidable economic and social barriers and exclusive spirit of the fifteenth and sixteenth centuries had not yet developed. In these conditions, new communities sprang up — towns, companies of merchants, craft guilds, and universities — and in the atmosphere of the time they also sought to secure their rights as institutions and the protection of their members by charters of immunities and privileges. We must not allow twentieth-century egalitarianism to leave us bewildered and repelled when confronted by the spectacle of burgesses claiming exemption from market tolls, which everyone else had to pay, or university undergraduates relying on their privileges as clerics and as students to protect them from penalties to which townsmen might be subject for acts of violence in the same brawls. So far from seeing any merit in equality, Western Europe of the twelfth and thirteenth centuries was deeply imbued with the conviction of the rightness and necessity of social hierarchy, even to the point of justifying it, on religious and intellectual grounds, as part of the divine and natural order of the universe. Just as the institution of monarchy reflected the rule of the universe by one God, so the existence of privileged orders rested firmly on the basis of their differing functions in the body politic and their differing responsibilities to God. And in this world of monarchy, expanding but under law, and of privileged groups becoming more numerous and more powerful, it was highly necessary, in expediency as well as in law, for the prince to summon assemblies of the most important privileged groups or estates, to consult with them not only about grants of taxation, but about proposals of law or justice which might affect their privileged status, or their immunities. To such assemblies prelates and magnates could be summoned to attend in person; but the lower clergy, the lesser nobility, and the burgesses were too numerous to come as individuals. Hence developed the practice of representation, arising, it would seem, in part from the example of representation within the Church and in part from the obvious commonsense solution to the problem of getting a coherent answer from an active community on whom a demand is made from outside.

This crystallization of parliaments of estates took place not in a static but a dynamic society; and the character of these parliaments was deeply affected by the changing relationships of the ruler and the privileged estates. In some countries it was the estates that grew in power at the expense of the ruler. The most striking example of a country where this happened was, of course, Poland, where the nobility, already strongly entrenched in power and privilege in the fourteenth and fifteenth centuries, was by the seventeenth century not only dominant over the weakened towns, but victorious over a throne now filled wholly by election, occupied by kings at the mercy of the *Sejm,* or parliament, and leagues of the nobility, and diminished in power at every fresh accession.

But the general trend in Europe was the other way. Fortified by the growing prestige of Roman law, helped by the economic decline of the older aristocracy in many countries, the princes were aided by new developments in warfare which their resources enabled them to use more effectively than those of magnates. The rulers were further assisted by the conception of the Renaissance prince, which justified disregard of established rights by the plea of "reason of state" — a conception often rendered more palatable to public opinion by the memory of fifteenth-century strife and disorder. And Reformation and Counter-Reformation, in spite of sharpening the spirit of resistance, and sometimes strengthening the nobility by their acquisition of Church lands, on the whole weakened parliaments in relation to the princes. . . .

In this age when the tide was on the whole running in favour of the rulers, various weaknesses of the parliaments of estates could be exploited by the princes. Maturity and success had fostered in the estates a spirit of exclusive legalism and conservatism that was further increased by their sense of growing danger from the prince. . . .

Another feature of this newer Europe was the tendency for the coalescence of smaller units into larger ones, whether by conquest or by dynastic inheritance; and, where this happened, the ruler could often use the resources of one of his enlarged dominions to reduce the authority of the parliament in another. . . .

Lastly, one very common weakness of these European assemblies of estates in their later days was in the attitude of the constituents to their representatives. Mr. Gaines Post may be right in arguing that in the early summoning of representative assemblies, especially in Italy, Roman law and canon law were strong influences making for assimilation of delegates of estates to plenipotentiary attorneys representing their principals in a court of law. But, as Signor Leicht has remarked in another connection, "*Si deve distinguere il lato historico dal lato giuridico*" — we must distinguish the historical aspect from the judicial. Assemblies of estates were not merely courts of law; they had an important political aspect as well, and the estates were normally most reluctant to allow their delegates full powers to commit the estates to whatever action should be agreed on in common counsel. In England, this spirit was overcome by the exceptional strength of the monarchy and the unusually strong feeling of the community of all classes and all parts of the realm. On the continent, however, the custom of strict mandates grew stronger, instead of weaker, in many countries; and if a new situation arose, not covered by their instructions, delegates often had to refer back to their constituents. Even the mighty Philip II of Spain had to strive very hard, for decades, to get the "*poderes,*" or instructions to the *procuradores* (deputies) of the towns in the enfeebled Cortes of Castile, converted into what today would be called "blanket powers." This trait was at all times a drag on efficiency and adaptability; and in combination with the determination of the ordinary members of the various estates not to permit the smallest infringement of the privileges of their order, the result was to menace the continued existence of the estates in the last generations of the old régime. For though a ruler such as Joseph II, or a minister such as Turgot, might see that changed conditions and ideas called for some limitation or even abolition of privileges, their moves in this direction were hampered, until it was too late, by the opposition of the great bulk of the privileged groups who, with these ideas of strict delegation of powers, could either block action in the assembly of estates or indignantly resort to other forms of resistance if the assembly were ignored. . . .

To many observers, ever since 1789 the history of these older representative institutions of Europe has, at any rate in its later stages, seemed mainly a cautionary tale — an awful warning of the self-destroying and far-reaching consequences of selfishness, pride, oppression, obscurantism, and indifference to justice and human suffering. Certainly, the last chapters in the history of these older European parliaments do mostly bear out the negative point that if a group, class, or institution insists on the maintenance of unalterable privileges in spite of radical changes in society and in thought, it will court disorder. But this view needs no underlining.

There is, however, another aspect of the history of these older representative institutions which points to a more direct connection between their history and that of modern parliamentary government in the West, a more positive aspect which bears on a great problem of our time. Already over a century ago Alexis de Tocqueville foresaw the ultimate danger of the democratic urge to be, not confusion, but despotism; and we now wonder how to avoid complete subjection of body and mind to an omnipotent state. The connection between the independence of groups and associations, and independence of thought and action, was one of which men of the old régime were very conscious. Jean Bodin (1530–96) is probably now most generally well known for his view that in every state there must be a recognized legal sovereign; but it ought also to be remembered that he said "Do away with corporations and communities, and you ruin the state and turn it into a barbarous tyranny." The history of Europe before 1789 can furnish many instances where a government began by breaking the privileges of a religious community, a

social class, or an assembly of estates, in the name of unity, truth, justice, or efficiency, and ended by moulding not only that group but others to its will. Of course, assemblies of estates and the privileges of the orders they represented are as dead as the old régime; but if the state is not all-powerful and all-pervading in the countries of Western Europe or North America as it is in Soviet Russia, is this due primarily to written constitutional guarantees, accepted constitutional practices, or declarations of the rights of men? Is it not more fundamental that in these countries there are still important groupings of power independent of the state, drawing their authority, their basic rights, and their vitality from other sources, however much they co-operate with the government? What effective barrier would remain against the despotism of the state, whether exercised through democratic forms or not, without the existence of independent magnets of authority and loyalty, such as churches, trade unions, business associations, professional organizations, universities, the religious or national bonds of some minority group? What protection was afforded to human rights, freedom of thought or speech, or legal equality, in Nazi Germany, once the power of resistance of other political parties, Länder governments, trade unions, and churches had been broken? The men of the old estates sensed that there is no effective limit upon power but rival power; and there may be more connexion between the spirit of the old rallying cries of "the liberties of the Church!" or "the privileges of the estates!" and the vitality of parliamentary government in the contemporary Western world than it is now popular to admit.

# SUGGESTIONS FOR ADDITIONAL READING

England, through the vast French possessions of Angevin kings, was linked closely to Europe in the thirteenth and fourteenth centuries; parliamentary development should therefore be studied against the background of similar representative assemblies on the Continent. The best surveys of European history in these centuries are in the series, *Peuples et civilisations,* volumes VI and VII (Paris, 1931–1941), and in the *Cambridge Medieval History,* volumes VI and VII (Cambridge, 1929–1932). In the Cambridge History, the article by C. H. McIlwain, "Medieval Estates," VII, 664–715, is an outstanding comparative survey of English and continental representative institutions; similar in scope are R. Fawtier, *l'Europe occidental de 1270 à 1380,* part I (Paris, 1940), 233–259, and, now in the Bobbs-Merrill reprint series, R. H. Lord, "The Parliaments of the Middle Ages and the Early Modern Period," *Catholic Historical Review,* XVI (1930), 125–144. For detailed studies of medieval and early modern assemblies in England and on the Continent see the publications of the *International Commission for the History of Representative and Parliamentary Institutions,* begun in 1937 and at present numbering twenty-eight volumes. The entire series of *Etudes présentées à la Commission Internationale pour l'histoire des assemblées d'états* is listed in volume XXVIII, J. Roskell, *The Commons and Their Speakers in English Parliaments, 1376–1523* (Manchester, 1965). References to other basic works on European assemblies can be found in volume I of the *Rise of Modern Europe* series, E. P. Cheyney, *The Dawn of a New Era, 1250–1453* (New York, 1936, Harper Torchback edn., New York, 1962), and in T. N. Bisson, *Assemblies and Representation in Languedoc in the Thirteenth Century* (Princeton, 1964).

England in this period has been surveyed by two volumes in the *Oxford History of England:* Sir M. Powicke, *The Thirteenth Century, 1216–1307,* 2nd edn. (Oxford, 1962), and May McKisack, *The Fourteenth Century, 1307–1399* (Oxford, 1959). As do all books in that series, they contain complete bibliographies. Useful short surveys, recently published, are volumes three and four by D. M. Stenton and A. R. Myers in the *Pelican History of England,* volumes II and III by Christopher Brooke and George Holmes in the *Nelson History of England,* and volume I by C. Warren Hollister in *A History of England* (Boston, 1966). Among the many up-to-date one-volume constitutional histories are the books by Goldwin Smith, B. Lyon, and C. R. Lovell. Of the older histories, the student should still consult G. B. Adams (revised, R. L. Schuyler), J. E. A. Joliffe, T. P. Taswell-Langmead (revised, T. F. T. Plucknett), A. B. White, and of course, F. W. Maitland. G. O. Sayles, *Medieval Foundations of England* (London, 1948), emphasizes justice in early parliaments, but is an excellent interpretive work. Students will appreciate the author's sketches of the period source material which precede every section of the book. Bertie Wilkinson stresses politics in early parliaments in his *Constitutional History of Medieval England 1216–1399,* three volumes (Toronto, 1948–1958), yet this work has a unique value in the way in which select documents are related to the narrative. Wilkinson's volumes, and Carl Stephenson and F. G. Marcham's *Sources of English Constitutional History* (New York, 1937), give a representative selection in English of pertinent medieval documents. References to full document collections are listed at the end of this essay. G. L. Haskins, *The Growth of English Representative Government* (London and Philadelphia, 1948), provides a good introduction to the origins of parliament, and two books by Faith Thompson, *Magna Carta: Its Role in the Making of the English Constitution, 1300–1629* (Minneapolis, 1949), and *A Short History of Parliament, 1295–1642* (Minneapolis, 1953), carry events down to the seventeenth century.

For all the controversy which has raged around William Stubbs, *The Constitutional History of England,* 6th edn., three volumes (Oxford, 1903), this classic study is still indispensable, although it should be used with C. Petit-Dutaillis and G. Lefebvre, *Studies Supplementary to Stubbs' Constitutional History,* three volumes, trans. W. A. Waugh, W. E. Rhodes, M. I. E. Robertson, and R. F. Treharne (Manchester, 1908–1929). Volume III covers medieval parliaments. Selections from Stubbs' writings have been edited with a critical introduction by N. F. Cantor, *William Stubbs on the English Constitution* (New York, 1966). Other evaluations of Stubbs' work are Helen Cam, "Stubbs Seventy Years After," *Cambridge Historical Journal,* IX (1948), 129–147, Sir J. G. Edwards, *William Stubbs* (Historical Association, 1952), and the provocative interpretation by H. G. Richardson and G. O. Sayles, *The Governance of Medieval England from the Conquest to Magna Carta* (Edinburgh, 1963), pp. 1–21. For an iconoclastic treatment of Stubbs's parliamentary constitution, see the popular monograph by A. F. Pollard, *The Evolution of Parliament,* 2nd edn. (New York, 1926; Russell and Russell edn., New York, 1964).

The Whig theory of early parliaments presented by Stubbs and nineteenth-century writers Henry Hallam, T. B. Macaulay, E. A. Freeman, and J. R. Green, can be traced to the original seventeenth-century political Whigs. Historical writing in the seventeenth century is discussed in J. G. A. Pocock, *The Ancient Constitution and the Feudal Law* (Cambridge, 1957), and Quentin Skinner, "History and Ideology in the English Revolu-

tion," *The Historical Journal,* VIII (1965), 151–179. Two volumes in the *Problems in European Civilization* series, P. A. M. Taylor, *The Origins of the English Civil War: Conspiracy, Crusade, or Class Conflict?* (Boston, 1960), and Gerald Straka, *The Revolution of 1688: Whig Triumph or Palace Revolution?* (Boston, 1963), incorporate selections from participants in these political crises. Whig historiography has been subjected to intense criticism by H. Butterfield, *The Whig Interpretation of History* (London, 1931, Norton edn., New York, 1965).

Historians opposed to Stubbs and the Whig interpretation of medieval history have drawn inspiration from F. W. Maitland's careful description of the "council-in-parliament" in his introduction to the *Records of the Parliament Holden at Westminster . . . in the Thirty-third Year of the Reign of Edward I* (the *Memoranda de Parliamento, 1305*), edited for the Rolls Series in 1893. Maitland's introduction has been reprinted in *Selected Historical Essays of F. W. Maitland,* ed. Helen Cam (Cambridge, 1957), pp. 52–96, and *Maitland: Selected Essays,* ed. H. D. Hazeltine, G. T. Lapsley, and P. H. Winfield (Cambridge, 1937), pp. 13–72. Commentaries on Maitland can be found in these books, together with R. L. Schuyler, "The Historical Spirit Incarnate F. W. Maitland," *American Historical Review,* LVII (1952), 303–322, and H.E. Bell, *Maitland: A Critical Examination and Assessment* (Cambridge, Mass., 1965).

The first work to apply the Maitland approach to parliament, C. H. McIlwain, *The High Court of Parliament and Its Supremacy* (New Haven, 1910, Bailey Bros. and Swinfen edn., London, 1963), emphasized the fusion of legislative and judicial powers in medieval government; collateral studies of the council, the courts and the administration have also demonstrated the fusion of powers. For the council, see J. F. Baldwin, *The King's Council During the Middle Ages* (Oxford, 1913), and A. B. White, "Was There a 'Common Council' Before Parliament," *American Historical Review,* XXV (1919), 1–17; for the administration see T. F. Tout, *Chapters in the Administrative History of Medieval England,* six volumes (Manchester, 1920–1933), and S. B. Chrimes, *An Introduction to the Administrative History of Medieval England* (Oxford, 1952). The impact of the exchequer court on parliamentary origins is measured by J. E. A. Joliffe, "Some Factors in the Beginnings of Parliament," *Transactions of the Royal Historical Society,* 4th Series, XXII (1940), 101–139. For the crucial role of royal officials, see H. G. Richardson and G. O. Sayles, "The King's Ministers in Parliament, 1272–1377," *English Historical Review,* XLVI (1931), 529–550, XLVII (1932), 194–203, 377–397. Judicial business in parliament is the recurring theme of H. G. Richardson and G. O. Sayles in a long series of publications beginning in 1928. In addition to their selection in this booklet, the reader should consult, "The Early Records of the English Parliaments, 1272–1377," *Bulletin of the Institute of Historical Research,* V (1928), 129–154, VI (1929), 71–88, 129–155, VIII (1931), 65–82, and IX (1932), 1–18, and "The Origins of Parliament," *Transactions of the Royal Historical Society,* 4th Series, XI (1928), 137–183.

There has been some hostile reaction to the degree of emphasis placed on judicial affairs in early parliaments. It is most extreme in Bertie Wilkinson, *Studies in the Constitutional History of the Thirteenth and Fourteenth Centuries,* 2nd edn. (Manchester, 1952), *The Constitutional History of England,* cited above, and two *Speculum* articles, "The 'Political Revolution' of the Thirteenth and Fourteenth Centuries in England," XXIV (1949), 502–509, and "English Politics and Politicians of the Thirteenth and Fourteenth Centuries," XXX (1955), 37–48. The judicial approach to parliament is challenged for the early thirteenth century by R. F. Treharne, "The Nature of Parliament in the Reign of Henry III," *English Historical Review,* LXXIV (1959), 590–610, and for Edward I's reign by Sir J. G. Edwards, " 'Justice' in Early English Parliaments," *Bulletin of the Institute of Historical Research,* XXVII (1954), 35–53. Significant also, are the conclusions for the first decade of Edward III's reign by T. F. T. Plucknett, "Parliament," *The English Government at Work, 1327–1336,* three volumes, ed. J. F. Willard and W. A. Morris (Cambridge, Mass., 1940–1950), I, 82–128.

The political struggle between Henry III and his barons should be studied for its impact on the origins of parliament. Charles Bémont, *Simon de Montfort,* trans. E. F. Jacob (Oxford, 1930) is still the best biography of the baronial leader, but it should be supplemented by H. Prentout's review of the Jacob edition, "Simon de Montfort et les origines du Parlement d'Angleterre; à propos du livre de C. Bémont," *Journal des savants,* XXIX (1930), 121–129, 158–164. See also, by R. F. Treharne, "The Personal Rule of Simon de Montfort in the Period of Baronial Reform and Rebellion, 1258–1265," *Proceedings of the British Academy,* XL (1955), 75–100, and *The Baronial Plan of Reform, 1258–1263* (Manchester, 1932), and by E. F. Jacob, *Studies in the Period of Baronial Reform and Rebellion, 1258–1267* (Oxford, 1925).

It is now clear that one cannot speak of a peerage or House of Lords until far into the fourteenth century. This is due in part to the pioneer work of J. H. Round, *Peerage and Pedigree,* two volumes (London, 1910). Other basic studies of the peerage are L. O. Pike, *The Constitutional History of the House of Lords* (London, 1894, Burt Franklin edn., New York, 1964), L. W. Vernon-Harcourt, *His Grace the Lord Steward and the Trial of Peers* (London, 1907), and recently, with a continental background, B. C. Kenney, *Judgment by Peers* (Cambridge, Mass., 1949). For the upper clergy, see H. M. Chew, *English Ecclesiastical Tenants-in-Chief and Knight Service, Especially in the Thirteenth and Fourteenth Centuries* (Oxford, 1932). W. A. Morris explores an important concept in "Magnates and Community of the Realm in Parliament, 1264–1327," *Medievalia et Humanistica,* I (1943), 58–94.

The once popular Stubbsian view that representation in England developed out of an urge in Anglo-Saxon blood has been rejected most strenuously by C. A. Beard, "The Teutonic Origins of Representative Government," *American Political Science Review,* XXVI (1932), 28–44. Still, the Anglo-Saxons are credited with creating agencies of local government which Anglo-Norman administrative genius used in implementing A. B. White's *Self-government at the King's Command* (Minneapolis and London, 1933). A recent treatment of the same theme is R. S. Hoyt, "Representation in the Administrative Practice of Anglo-Norman England," *Album Helen Maud Cam,* two volumes (Louvain, 1960–1961), II, 15–26. Anglo-Saxon institutional background is described by Helen Cam in *Studies in the Hundred Rolls* (Oxford, 1921), *The Hundred and the Hundred Rolls* (London, 1930), and in a long series of articles, most of which are reprinted in *Liberties and Communities in Medieval England* (Cambridge, 1944, Barnes, Noble, edn., New York, 1963), and *Law-finders and Law-makers in Medieval England* (New York, 1963). Volume I of *Album Helen Maud Cam,* above, contains a full bibliography of Miss Cam's publications.

The changing interpretations of Edward I in historical literature are reviewed by Geoffrey Templeman, "Edward I and the Historians," *Cambridge Historical Journal,* X (1950), 16–35, and V. H. Galbraith, "Good Kings and Bad Kings in Medieval English History," *History,* XXX (1945), 119–132. Sir Maurice Powicke, *King Henry III and the Lord Edward,* two volumes (London, 1947), shows unusual insight into the human motivations of feudal society. For a recent hostile view of Edward, see K. B. McFarlane, "Had

Edward I a 'Policy' Towards the Earls," *History,* L (1965), 145–149. The abiding money crisis in Edward's reign led to a struggle with the barons, which, according to the traditional Stubbs view, was resolved by the king's acknowledgment, in the Confirmation of the Charters, 1297, of the tax-granting rights of parliament. This view of the Charters is challenged by H. Rothwell in two articles, "The Confirmation of the Charters, 1297," *English Historical Review,* LX (1945), 16–35, 177–191, 300–315, and "Edward I and the Struggle for the Charters, 1297–1305," *Studies in Medieval History Presented to F. M. Powicke,* ed. R. W. Hunt, W. A. Pantin, R. W. Southern (Oxford, 1948), pp. 319–332. Edward I's parliamentary taxation is viewed not as a crisis policy but as a consciously planned program of enlarging the community of the realm by R. S. Hoyt, *The Royal Demesne in English Constitutional History* (Cornell, 1950). Regardless of Edward's motivation, the importance of taxation as a factor in parliamentary origins is no longer disputed. Basic studies of tax procedures are J. F. Willard, *Parliamentary Taxes on Personal Property, 1290–1334* (Cambridge, Mass., 1934), May McKisack, *The Parliamentary Representation of the English Boroughs during the Middle Ages* (London, 1932, F. Cass edn., London, 1962), S. K. Mitchell *Taxation in Medieval England,* ed. Sidney Painter (Yale, 1951), and two articles by Carl Stephenson, "Taxation and Representation in the Middle Ages," and "The Beginnings of Representative Government in England," both of which are reprinted in *Medieval Institutions: Selected Essays,* ed. Bryce D. Lyon (Cornell, 1954).

It was taken for granted by nineteenth-century historians that early parliaments "legislated" in the modern sense; but C. H. McIlwain argued in 1910 that medieval parliaments could do no more than enact existing customs which resided in the "fundamental law." McIlwain's emphasis on the fundamental law provoked controversy and stimulated new research on the medieval law making process. The important studies are J. W. Gough, *Fundamental Law in English Constitutional History* (Oxford, 1955), T. F. T. Plucknett, *Statutes and Their Interpretation in the First Half of the Fourteenth Century* (Cambridge, 1922), and *The Legislation of Edward I* (Oxford, 1949), H. G. Richardson and G. O. Sayles, "The Early Statutes," *Law Quarterly Review,* I (1934), 201–223, 540–571, and Geoffrey Barraclough, "Law and Legislation in Medieval England," *Law Quarterly Review,* LVI (1940), 75–92. See also, F. Pollock and F. W. Maitland, *The History of English Law Before the Time of Edward I,* two volumes (Cambridge, 1895), and W. S. Holdsworth, *The History of English Law,* twelve volumes (London, 1922–1938). The European scene is covered by Fritz Kern, *Kingship and Law in the Middle Ages,* trans. S. B. Chrimes (Oxford, 1939).

Maitland's detailed analysis of the petitioning process in the 1305 parliament convinced many historians that representatives came primarily to seek judicial relief in the king's highest court. The theory was originally stated by Ludwig Riess in 1885 and 1888: *The History of the English Electoral Law in the Middle Ages,* trans. and ed. K. L. Wood-Legh (Cambridge, 1940), and "Der Ursprung des englischen Unterhauses," *Historische Zeitschrift,* IX (1888), 1–33. D. Pasquet, in the selection included in this booklet, expands the Riess petitioning concept to incude the theory that Edward used representatives as part of a plan to destroy feudalism. G. L. Haskins, on the other hand, in "The Petitions of Representatives in the Parliaments of Edward I," *English Historical Review,* LIII (1938), 1–20, shows that representatives did not petition in the way suggested by Riess and Pasquet. Closely connected to the petitioning theory was the assumption that petitions, particularly "common petitions," had developed into statute legislation early in the fourteenth century. Several publications have called this assumption premature, among them, H. L. Gray, *The Influence of the Commons on Early Legislation* (Harvard, 1932), Doris Rayner, "The Forms and Machinery of the 'Commune Petition' in the Fourteenth Century," *English Historical Review,* LVI (1941), 198–233, 549–570, and Helen Cam, "The Legislators of Medieval England," *Proceedings of the British Academy,* XXXI (1947), 127–150.

Motives of propaganda and habits of military organization have also been suggested as explanations for the summons of representatives. Helen Cam's observations on the propaganda motive are included in this booklet; the reader should consult, in addition, J. R. Strayer, "The Statute of York and the Community of the Realm," *American Historical Review,* XLVII (1941), 1–22. The relationship between military service and the origins of representation is noted by T. N. Bisson, "Military Origins of Medieval Representation," *American Historical Review,* LXXI (1966), 1199–1218. See also B. C. Keeney, "Military Service and the Development of Nationalism in England, 1272–1327," *Speculum,* XXII (1947), 534–549, and M. R. Powicke, *Military Obligation in Medieval England* (New York, 1962).

Sir Ernest Barker pointed to the Church as a factor in the origins of representation and this theme is developed in Maude V. Clarke's important study, *Medieval Representation and Consent* (London, 1936, Russell and Russell edn., New York, 1964). Covering other aspects of the church and representation are G. R. Galbraith, *The Constitution of the Dominican Order* (Manchester, 1925), W. E. Lunt, *The Valuation of Norwich* (Oxford, 1926), Sir Maurice Powicke, *Stephen Langton* (Oxford, 1928, Barnes, Noble, edn., New York, 1964), and D. B. Weske, "The Attitude of the English Clergy in the Thirteenth and Fourteenth Centuries Towards the Obligation of Attendance on Convocations and Parliaments," *Essays in History and Political Theory in Honor of*

*C. H. McIlwain* (Harvard, 1936), pp. 77–108.

The case for Roman Law as an important root of representation in Europe and England has been put effectively by Gaines Post in a number of articles on the *plena potestas* and *quod omnes tangit* formulas. Nearly all have been reprinted in Post's *Studies in Medieval Legal Thought: Public Law and the State, 1100–1322* (Princeton, 1964). The book has a detailed bibliography.

Post's work is in part an answer to Sir J. G. Edwards, "The 'Plena Potestas' of English Parliamentary Representatives," *Oxford Essays to H. E. Salter* (Oxford, 1934), pp. 141–154, which describes *plena potestas* as a political rather than a legal formula. In the selection in this booklet and in *The Commons in Medieval English Parliaments* (London, 1958), Edwards examines the degree of the representatives' participation, suggesting that their role in parliament has been undervalued by historians.

Published documents relating to early parliaments include parliamentary rolls and a wide variety of administrative and legal records, only a few of which can be indicated here. For a more extensive listing, see Sir Maurice Powicke's *Thirteenth Century* and May McKisack's *Fourteenth Century,* cited above. Parliamentary rolls were first published as *Rotuli Parliamentorum,* six volumes, ed. J. Strachey and others (London, 1767), and have been supplemented by *Documents Illustrative of English History in the Thirteenth and Fourteenth Centuries,* ed. Henry Cole (Record Commission, 1844), the *Memoranda de Parliamento,* cited above, and *Rotuli Parliamentorum Anglie Hactenus Inediti,* ed. H. G. Richardson and G. O. Sayles (Camden Society, 1928). For chronicles and the Year Books (summaries of cases tried in the king's courts, compiled in the period 1292–1535) see the publications of the Royal Historical Society, Camden Series (London, 1838–), the Selden Society (London, 1887–), and the *Chronicles and Memorials of Great Britain and Ireland during the Middle Ages,* 254 volumes (London, 1858–1911), more commonly known as the Rolls Series. All of these document collections contain important introductions by Stubbs, Maitland, and others. Guides to the documents are W. C. Bolland, *Manual of Year Book Studies* (Cambridge, 1925), V. H. Galbraith, *An Introduction to the Use of the Public Records* (Oxford, 1934), *Guide to the Contents of the Public Record Office,* two volumes (H. M. Stationery Office, 1963), A. K. R. Kiralfy and G. H. Jones, *General Guide to the Society's Publications,* volumes I–LXXIX (Selden Society, 1960), W. S. Holdsworth, *Sources and Literature of English Law* (Oxford, 1925), and P. H. Winfield, *The Chief Sources of English Legal History* (Cambridge, 1925).

Students of the Medieval English parliament will want to pursue the subject beyond the reign of Edward I into the fourteenth and fifteenth centuries, considering, in Edward II's reign, the baronial crises which issued in the controversial Statute of York; in Edward III's reign, the emergence of the commons, with their speaker, the hammering out of impeachment procedure, and the first gropings toward parliamentary privilege; and in Henry IV's reign, the premature experiments at controlling the king's council, the royal expenditure, and the wording of statutes. Bibliographical information for the whole spectrum of medieval parliamentary history can be found in G. T. Lapsley, "Some Recent Advance in English Constitutional History (Before 1485)," *Crown, Community, and Parliament in the Later Middle Ages,* ed. Helen Cam and Geoffrey Barraclough (Oxford, 1951), pp. 1–33, Geoffrey Templeman, "The History of Parliament to 1400 in the Light of Modern Research," *The Making of English History,* ed. R. L. Schuyler and H. Ausubel (New York, 1952), pp. 109–127, R. S. Hoyt, "Recent Publications in the United States and Canada in the History of

Western and Representative Institutions Before the French Revolution," *Speculum,* XXIX (1954), 356–366, Edward Miller, *The Origins of Parliament* (Historical Association, 1960), Sir J. G. Edwards, *Historians and the Medieval English Parliament* (Glasgow, 1960), Margaret Hastings, "High History or Hack History: England in the Later Middle Ages," *Speculum,* XXXVI (1961), 225–263, and G. P. Cuttino, "Medieval Parliament Reinterpreted," *Speculum,* XLI (1966), 681–687.